ITALIAN COOKING SCHOOL

DESSERTS

ITALIAN COOKING SCHOOL

DESSERTS

THE SILVER SPOON KITCHEN

ART OF BAKING

It comes as no surprise to see the resurgence of baking over recent years. For some, the act of baking is a creative outlet primed for experimenting; for others, it's an age-old hobby that can evoke the nostalgia of yesteryear. Baking is one of those rare crafts that is generally experienced with others and allows us to find generosity in ourselves and nurture relationships with friends and family.

And when it comes to deciding what to bake, bakers often turn to recipes that offer the greatest source of comfort: classic cakes, seasonal pies, and traditional cookies. Baking is an exploration of the imagination. Apples, mixed berries, chocolate, or custard—so many inviting ingredients can take center stage in tarts, pies, and strudels and enjoyed by both adults and children alike.

Italian Cooking School Desserts features 75 recipes for baking delicious home-baked desserts to fit every occasion. The book is designed with the beginner in mind, offering readers everything they need to know to create cookies, cakes, tarts, and filled pastries. Start by following the step-by-steps for basic recipes and once mastered, find inspiration in the collection of baked goods such as Amaretti Cookies (see page 20) and Mocha Cake with Rum (see page 96). By the time you've worked through the entire book, you should be well-versed in the art of baking.

Moreover, a basics section details essential ingredients, utensils, and culinary shortcuts to wrangle the best results from your efforts. From Sicilian Almond Cookies (see page 44) to Ricotta and Cherry Strudel (see page 155) to a Pistachio and Chocolate Pie (see page 176), *Italian Cooking School Desserts* offers a delectable range of classic and contemporary baked desserts.

THE DESSERTS

COOKIES

Cookies (biscuits) were pieces of bread that had been cooked twice. By the Middle Ages, they were sweetened with honey and had grown in popularity. and today, they are favorite snack around the world. Many of the cookie recipes in this book are regional specialties: canestrelli (Liguria and Piedmont), cantuccini (Prato in Tuscany), and baci di dama (Tortona in Piedmont).

CAKES

The book features a range of round and tube-shaped cakes. A typical cake recipe starts with five ingredients: flour, eggs, sugar, butter, and a leavener (raising agent), with other ingredients added for taste and/or color—from a simple Lemon Cake (see page 80) to a chocolate Marbled Cake (see page 87).

TARTS

A tart can be defined as an open pastry shell (case) containing a sweet or savory filling. The pastry is usually basic pie dough, or shortcrust pastry, and the filling is often based on fruit or custard. Tartlets, such as the Lemon and Kiwi Tartlets (see page 108), are miniature tarts that can be made using smaller pans and molds.

FILLED PASTRIES

Filled pastries include pies and strudels. A pie is essentially a tart with a pastry lid and can be prepared with a decorative lattice pattern (Cherry Pie, see page 151) or a solid top (Spongata from Pontremoli, see page 172). With the latter, it is important to seal the edges well and to prick the lid in order for steam to escape during the baking process. Although strudel is often associated with countries such as Austria and Germany, it is a typical dessert of Alto Adige, a northern Italian region. Strudel originated in the Middle Ages as a variation on a sweet mixture of dried fruit, nuts, bread, and liqueur and the Italian version is often made with thinly rolled puff pastry that has been stuffed with fruit.

INGREDIENTS

FLOUR

Flour is the foundation for all baked goods from cookies and cakes to tarts and pies. All-purpose (plain) flour is most commonly used. Whole wheat (wholemeal) flour creates a dense texture and is seldom used in baked desserts. A leavener (or raising agent) can be added to all-purpose flour to create a rise in some recipes.

LEAVENERS

Baking soda (bicarbonate of soda), which needs an acid and moisture to activate it, has a strong flavor and should be used sparingly. Baking powder is comprised of baking soda and cream of tartar (an acid that helps to release the carbon dioxide in the baking soda and aerate the cake with moisture). A leavener should be sifted with other dry ingredients so it is evenly distributed into the mixture. A pinch of baking soda or baking powder may be added to a recipe to make the pastry softer.

BUTTER

Butter is an essential ingredient, because it imparts a rich, distinctive flavor to baked desserts. When making a cake, butter is beaten together with sugar to incorporate air into the mixture and produces a light, fluffy batter.

SUGAR

Superfine (caster) sugar, which dissolves quickly, is ideal for desserts. (In fact, if you need superfine, you can process granulated white sugar into a food processor for 30 seconds). Confectioners' (icing) sugar is useful for icings, frostings, and simple dusting of cakes. A variety of brown sugars, which can be found in fruit or richly flavored cakes, is also useful to have in the pantry.

VANILLA

When it comes to vanilla extract, invest in the real deal, which is made from vanilla beans and is far superior in flavor than vanilla essence.

EGGS

Eggs give moisture and act as a leavener and binder. Brush the tart's edges, decorative strips of pastry, and cookies with a beaten egg for a shiny glaze.

BASIC PIE DOUGH (SHORTCRUST PASTRY)

Before anyone can think about any type of filling, a pie or tart begins with the dough, and more specifically, the basic pie dough (shortcrust pastry), for which there are many variations. When tarts and pies have a wet filling (such as fruit ones, or those with a filling of chocolate cream), "blind baking" is often recommended to precook the pastry and to prevent the pie crust from becoming soggy once it's filled. Simply roll out the dough, transfer it to a baking pan or pie plate, prick it with the prongs of a fork, cover it with parchment (baking) paper, and spread a layer of pie weights (baking beans) on top. Bake it in the oven preheated to 350–400°F/180–200°C/ Gas Mark 4–6, for about 20 minutes, then remove the paper and weights, and let cool before filling it.

Avoid using preserve, jam, or jelly that is too runny, which could cause the pastry to become soggy or damp. Spread out the jam in the pastry shell (case), smooth it out evenly with a spatula, then place the pastry lid or strips on top and bake in the oven.

YOGURT, RICOTTA, AND MASCARPONE CHEESES

Tart fillings can also be dairy based and filled with other ingredients, such as dried fruit, nuts, fresh fruit, chocolate, or preserves.

CHOCOLATE

Chocolate is another classic baking ingredients: it can be added for texture, flavor, or pure indulgence.

FRESH FRUIT

Seasonal fruit should be arranged imaginatively on a layer of pastry cream or jam. To make the fruit appear more glossy, brush it with a layer of gelatin (made with gelatin sheets [leaves] or by heating preserves or jam with the juice of half an orange, a little water, and some powdered gelatin) or melted jelly.

EQUIPMENT

BAKING PANS FOR TARTS

The pans used in this book are usually round in shape, shallow with smooth or fluted edges and 9½–10 inches/ 24–25 cm in diameter. They are usually made from a nonstick material such as silicone, and where indicated, grease and dust a baking pan or line it with parchment (baking) paper before placing the dough inside. Springform pans are very useful, because they have sides that can be unclipped to make removing the tart easier. Alternatively, pans with removable bottoms can also be used.

LOAF PANS AND TUBE PANS

In addition to round baking pans, the baker should also have a rectangular loaf pan and a Bundt pan or tube pan (ring mold). These can be made from a nonstick material, such as silicone.

COOKIE CUTTERS

Nowadays, cookie cutters come in all shapes and sizes, from simple geometric ones to more elaborate and decorative designs for special occasions and holidays such as Christmas, Valentine's Day, and Halloween.

PASTRY (PIPING) BAG

This is a conical bag (made from disposable plastic, silicone, or a similar material) to give shape to small cookies. Each one requires an appropriate tip (nozzle) of the correct size, which can be smooth or shaped.

SMALL UTENSILS

Some tools are simply indispensable in pastry making and include: a whisk to mix and work the ingredients; a rolling pin to roll out pastry; a scraper to cut dough; a knife to cut strips for a pie lid; a spatula to smooth and level custards; and a pastry brush with which to apply egg wash to the dough before it is baked.

COOKIES

TECHNIQUE

EASY

– Preparation time: *15 minutes*
– Cooking time: *20 minutes*
– Calories per cookie: *120*
– *Makes 18*

INGREDIENTS

– 7 tablespoons (3½ oz/100 g) butter
– ½ vanilla bean
– 6 tablespoons (3 oz/80 g) sugar
– ¾ cup (3½ oz/100 g) all-purpose (plain) flour
– ½ cup (2 oz/50 g) cornstarch (cornflour)
– 1 teaspoon baking powder
– 1 egg, lightly beaten
– ⅓ cup (2 oz/50 g) chocolate chips
– salt

STEP 1

Preheat the oven to 350°F/180°C/Gas Mark 4 and line a baking sheet with parchment (baking) paper. Melt the butter over very low heat and let cool. Split the vanilla bean lengthwise, scrape out the seeds, and add to the butter. Stir the sugar into the butter mixture. In a large bowl, sift the flour with the cornstarch (cornflour) and the baking powder and add the salt.

STEP 2

Add the egg and melted butter to the flour mixture and stir well to combine. Add the chocolate chips and stir again to combine.

STEP 3

Using 2 teaspoons, or a cookie scoop, put small mounds of the dough onto the baking sheet, set 1 inch/2.5 cm apart. Flatten slightly with your palm.

STEP 4

Bake for about 20 minutes or until light brown around the edges and just set in the center. The cookies (biscuits) will spread a little during cooking and take on their typical wafer-like appearance. Let cool before serving.

AMARETTI

AMARETTI COOKIES

EASY

- Preparation time: *50 minutes*
- Cooking time: *15 minutes*
- Calories per cookie: *40*
- *Makes 60*

INGREDIENTS

- 1⅔ cups (5 oz/150 g) chopped almonds
- generous ½ cup (4 oz/110 g) sugar
- 4 egg whites
- 2 cups (8 oz/240 g) confectioners' (icing) sugar, sifted
- ½ teaspoon vanilla extract

Preheat the oven to 350°F/180°C/Gas Mark 4 and line a baking sheet with parchment (baking) paper. Grind the almonds in a blender for no longer than 1 minute, then add the sugar and blend for another 2 minutes. Process until everything is finely ground and transfer to a bowl.

Whisk the egg whites to stiff peaks, then gradually add the confectioners' (icing) sugar, continuing to whisk the mixture until it is firm and glossy. Add the vanilla extract, mixing gently, then fold in the ground almonds a little at a time.

Put the dough into a pastry (piping) bag fitted with a plain ½-inch/1-cm tip (nozzle) and pipe little mounds, about 1 inch/2.5 cm high, on the parchment paper, about 1 inch/2.5 cm apart. Dust with confectioners' sugar and let stand for 10–15 minutes.

Bake for about 15 minutes, or until puffed up and lightly browned. Remove and let cool completely, then remove them from the paper. They can be stored in an airtight container.

Tip: For an irresistible treat, melt 3½ oz/100 g semisweet (dark) chocolate in a double boiler or heatproof bowl set over a saucepan of barely simmering water. Spoon the chocolate onto the flat side of a cookie (biscuit), then top with another cookie to make a little sandwich.

BISCOTTI FROLLINI

SHORTBREAD COOKIES

EASY

– Preparation time: *15 minutes*
– Cooking time: *12 minutes*
– Calories per cookie: *92*
– *Makes 18*

INGREDIENTS

– 3 hard-boiled egg yolks
– ¼ cup (2 oz/50 g) sugar
– 7 tablespoons (3½ oz/100 g) butter
– scant 1 cup (3½ oz/100 g) all-purpose (plain) flour, plus extra for dusting
– ⅓ cup (2 oz/50 g) potato flour
– pearl sugar, for decoration (optional)
– confectioners' (icing) sugar, for dusting

Preheat the oven to 350°F/180°C/Gas Mark 4 and line a baking sheet with parchment (baking) paper. Push the egg yolks through a strainer (sieve) and use a spatula to beat them with the sugar and butter in a bowl. Sift in both flours and stir them in until just combined. This mixture needs to be kept as cool as possible; too much handling will adversely affect the end result.

Roll out the dough into a thick sheet on a lightly floured surface, and use a fluted pastry wheel to cut it into a 2½ x ¾ inch/6 x 2 cm rectangle. Place them on the prepared baking sheet, decorate each cookie (biscuit) with pearl sugar, if using, and bake for 12 minutes.

Dust with confectioners' (icing) sugar and serve.

CANESTRELLI

DAISY COOKIES

EASY

– Preparation time: *45 minutes
  + 30 minutes chilling*
– Cooking time: *8–10 minutes*
– Calories per cookie: *112*
– *Makes 24*

INGREDIENTS

– 2⅓ cups (11 oz/300 g)
  all-purpose (plain) flour,
  sifted, plus extra for dusting
– 1¼ sticks (5 oz/150 g) butter
– scant ½ cup (3 oz/90 g)
  sugar
– 1 whole egg plus 1 egg
  separated
– confectioners' (icing) sugar,
  for dusting

Preheat the oven to 375°F/190°C/Gas Mark 5 and line a baking sheet with parchment (baking) paper. Put the flour, butter, and sugar into a bowl and rub the butter into the flour until it resembles coarse bread crumbs. Add the whole egg and egg yolk and quickly combine with your hands to make a soft dough. Roll it out on a lightly floured surface to a thickness of ½ inch/1 cm.

Using a round, scalloped-edge pastry cutter, cut out daisy shapes with a hole in the middle, place them on the baking sheet, and chill in the refrigerator for at least 30 minutes.

Lightly beat the egg white and brush the cookies (biscuits) with it, then bake for 8–10 minutes, or until golden brown. Remove, let cool, then dust liberally with confectioners' (icing) sugar.

GIALLETTI

CORNMEAL AND LEMON COOKIES

EASY

– Preparation time: *20 minutes
  + 1 hour chilling*
– Cooking time: *15–20 minutes*
– Calories per cookie: *67*
– *Makes 27*

INGREDIENTS

– butter, for greasing
– 1 cup (5 oz/50 g) superfine
  cornmeal
– 1¼ cups (5 oz/150 g)
  all-purpose (plain) flour
– 4 teaspoons baking powder
– 1 whole egg plus 1 egg yolk
– ¾ cup (5 oz/150 g) superfine
  (caster) sugar
– grated zest of 1 unwaxed
  lemon
– milk, as needed

Preheat the oven to 350°F/180°C/Gas Mark 4 and grease a baking sheet. Sift together the cornmeal, flour, and baking powder into a large bowl and make a well in the center. Break the whole egg into it, add the egg yolk, ½ cup (3½ oz/100 g) sugar, the lemon zest, and just enough milk to bring it together into a soft, smooth dough. Shape into a ball, wrap in plastic wrap (clingfilm), and chill in the refrigerator for about 1 hour.

Shape the dough into walnut-size balls, flatten them slightly, and shape each one so that they are slightly elongated. Space them out on the baking sheet, dust with the remaining sugar, and bake for 15–20 minutes. Remove, let cool, and serve.

MORETTI AL PROFUMO D'ARANCIA

CHOCOLATE AND ORANGE COOKIES

EASY

– Preparation time: *20 minutes plus 1 hour chilling*
– Cooking time: *15 minutes*
– Calories per cookie: *133*
– *Makes 25*

INGREDIENTS

– 3½ oz/100 g semisweet (dark) chocolate, grated
– 2⅓ cups (10 oz/280 g) all-purpose (plain) flour, plus extra for dusting
– 1 stick (4 oz/120 g) butter, softened, cut into small pieces
– ⅔ cup (4 oz/120 g) granulated sugar
– 1 tablespoon unsweetened cocoa powder, sifted
– grated zest of 1 unwaxed orange
– 2 eggs plus 1 egg yolk
– pearl sugar, to decorate

Melt the chocolate in a double boiler or a heatproof bowl set over a saucepan of simmering water. Stir, then let cool to room temperature.

Sift the flour into a large bowl, make a well in the center, and add the butter, sugar, chocolate, cocoa powder, orange zest, 1 whole egg, and 1 egg yolk. Mix the ingredients into the flour to make a soft dough. If necessary, knead the dough slightly to achieve an even consistency.

Place the dough between two layers of plastic wrap (clingfilm) and roll into a disk, ⅛ inch/3 mm thick, and chill for about 1 hour, until firm.

Preheat the oven to 350°F/180°C/Gas Mark 4 and line a baking sheet with parchment (baking) paper. Cut out with cookie cutters, using different shapes, if desired. Transfer to the baking sheet.

In a small bowl, beat the remaining egg. Brush the cookies (biscuits) with the egg, decorate the centers with pearl sugar, and bake for about 15 minutes. Remove, let stand on a baking sheet for 1 minute, then transfer to a wire rack to cool before serving.

Tip: If you cannot find pearl sugar, coarsely crush some sugar cubes in a metal bowl, using the end of a rolling pin.

MEZZELUNE DI PASTA FROLLA

HALF MOON COOKIES

EASY

– Preparation time: *15 minutes*
– Cooking time: *12 minutes*
– Calories per cookie: *117*
– *Makes 30*

INGREDIENTS

– ¾ quantity Basic Pie Dough (Shortcrust Pastry), see page 105
– 2⅓ cups (7 oz/200 g) ground almonds (almond meal)
– 4 tablespoons confectioners' (icing) sugar
– ½ cup (2 oz/50 g) vanilla sugar, for dusting (see tip)
– multicolor sugar sprinkles, for decorating (optional)

Preheat the oven to 375°F/180°C/Gas Mark 5 and line a baking sheet with parchment (baking) paper. Knead the dough very briefly, add the ground almonds, and continue to knead until it's incorporated.

Divide the dough into 30 pieces, then shape each piece into a cylinder, 1 inch/2.5 cm thick and ¾ inch/2 cm long. Roll each cylinder in the palms of your hands to make it longer, then press it into a half-moon shape. Repeat this process.

Transfer to the baking sheet, sprinkle the cookies (biscuits) with multicolor sugar sprinkles, if using, and press in lightly. Bake for 10–12 minutes or until lightly golden on the edges. Remove the cookies and while they are still warm, dust them with the vanilla sugar. Arrange on a dish and serve.

Tip: To make vanilla sugar, combine confectioners' (icing) sugar with the seeds from a vanilla bean, or store the sugar in a jar with a slit vanilla bean for about a week. A variety of sugars can be used to make vanilla sugar for other recipes.

BISCOTTI ALLE NOCCIOLE

HAZELNUT COOKIES

EASY

– Preparation time: *10 minutes*
– Cooking time: *10 minutes*
– Calories per serving: *103*
– *Makes 30*

INGREDIENTS

– 7 oz/200 g (1⅔ cups)
  all-purpose (plain) flour
– 1 egg, lightly beaten
– ¾ cup (5½ oz/160 g)
  superfine (caster) sugar
– ¾ cup (3½ oz/100 g)
  coarsely chopped hazelnuts
– ½ cup (3½ oz/100 g)
  chocolate chips
– 6 tablespoons (3 oz/80 g)
  butter, melted and cooled

Preheat the oven to 350°F/180°C/Gas Mark 4 and line a baking sheet with parchment (baking) paper.

Sift the flour into a large bowl and make a well in the center. Add the egg, then add the sugar, hazelnuts, and chocolate chips. Slowly pour in the melted butter and mix gently with a fork.

Take a little of the dough at a time and shape into flattened balls. Arrange them on the baking sheet and bake for 10 minutes. Remove and let cool, then place on a serving dish and serve or store for a few days in an airtight container.

BRUTTI MA BUONI

UGLY-BUT-GOOD COOKIES

EASY

– Preparation time: *20 minutes*
– Cooking time: *50 minutes*
– Calories per cookie: *56*
– *Makes 50*

INGREDIENTS

– 1 cup (5 oz/150 g) skinless almonds
– 1 cup (5 oz/150 g) skinless hazelnuts
– 3 egg whites
– 1 cup (7 oz/200 g) sugar
– pinch of ground cinnamon

Preheat the oven to 400°F/200°C/Gas Mark 6. Toast the almonds and hazelnuts in the oven for about 5 minutes, or until golden. Remove and let cool, then chop them coarsely. Reduce the oven temperature to 285°F/140°C/Gas Mark 1 and line a baking sheet with parchment (baking) paper.

Whisk the egg whites to stiff peaks using an electric mixer, then gradually beat in the sugar to make a glossy, firm meringue.

Add the chopped nuts and cinnamon and fold in with a spatula. Transfer the mixture to a heatproof bowl and place it over a saucepan of barely simmering water for about 15 minutes, stirring frequently, until slightly thickened.

Using 2 teaspoons, or a cookie scoop, place little mounds of the dough on the prepared baking sheet and bake for about 30 minutes.

Tip: To make the cookies (biscuits) with a little more spice, add ½ teaspoon ground ginger and some ground allspice.

BISCOTTI ALLO ZENZERO

GINGER SHORTBREAD COOKIES

EASY

– Preparation time: *15 minutes*
– Cooking time: *10–15 minutes*
– Calories per cookie: *160*
– *Makes 18*

INGREDIENTS

– 1 stick (4 oz/125 g) butter,
  softened
– 2 teaspoons finely grated
  fresh ginger
– ½ cup (2 oz/50 g)
  confectioners' (icing) sugar
– 1½ cups (7 oz/200 g)
  all-purpose (plain) flour,
  plus extra for dusting

Preheat the oven to 350°F/180°C/Gas Mark 4 and line a baking sheet with parchment (baking) paper. In a large bowl, beat the butter and ginger until creamy, then add the sugar. Stir in the flour a little at a time, then add a little lukewarm water, if necessary, to make a soft dough.

Roll out the dough on a lightly floured surface into a disk, ½ inch/1 cm thick, then cut the dough into small disks 2 inches/5 cm in diameter. Place on the baking sheet and chill until firm. Bake for 10–15 minutes, until lightly browned.

Remove and let cool before serving. They will also keep well for several days in an airtight container.

BISCOTTI SPEZIATI

SPICED COOKIES

EASY

– Preparation time: *20 minutes*
  + 12 hours resting
– Cooking time: *15 minutes*
– Calories per cookie: 162
– *Makes 24*

INGREDIENTS

– 2 cups (9 oz/250 g)
  all-purpose (plain) flour
– scant 1 cup (6½ oz/180 g)
  sugar
– 1 teaspoon baking soda
  (bicarbonate of soda)
– 1½ teaspoons ground
  cinnamon
– 1 teaspoon ground ginger
– ½ teaspoon ground nutmeg
– 1 egg, lightly beaten, plus
  1 egg white
– generous 1¼ sticks
  (5½ oz/160 g) butter, melted
– 2¼ cups (9 oz/250 g)
  confectioners' (icing) sugar
– a few drops of lemon juice
– pinch of salt

Preheat the oven to 350°F/180°C/Gas Mark 4 and line a baking sheet with parchment (baking) paper. Sift the flour into a bowl and stir in the sugar, baking soda (bicarbonate of soda), spices, and a pinch of salt. Add the whole egg and the butter and stir well to combine. Wrap it in plastic wrap (clingfilm) and rest in the refrigerator for 12 hours.

Roll out the dough, about ⅛ inch/3 mm thick, and cut out different shapes with a cookie cutter. Transfer to the baking sheet and bake for about 15 minutes.

Transfer the cookies (biscuits) to a cooling rack and let cool. Sift the confectioners' (icing) sugar. Place the egg white in a bowl and beat with a fork to froth it lightly. Add a couple of drops of lemon juice. Gradually stir in the confectioners' sugar to make a soft piping consistency. Using a piping (pastry) bag fitted with a small nozzle (tip), decorate them with the icing.

- Preparation time: *40 minutes + 2 hours soaking time and 1 hour chilling time*
- Cooking time: *12–15 minutes*
- Calories per cookie: *124*
- *Makes 40*

INGREDIENTS

- ⅔ cup (3½ oz/100 g) raisins
- scant 1 cup (7 fl oz/200 ml) grappa or brandy
- 2 egg yolks
- 1 cup (7 oz/200 g) sugar
- 1¼ sticks (5 oz/150 g) butter, softened
- ⅓ cup (2½ oz/70 g) soft lard
- grated zest of 1 unwaxed lemon
- few drops of vanilla extract
- generous 2 cups (11 oz/ 300 g) fine cornmeal
- 1⅓ cups (5 oz/150 g) all-purpose (plain) flour
- 1¼ teaspoons baking powder
- salt
- confectioners' (icing) sugar, for dusting (optional)
- zabaglione (see page 123), to serve (optional)

Soak the raisins in the grappa for about 2 hours to soften and absorb the flavor.

Whisk the egg yolks and the sugar in a bowl until pale and fluffy, then beat in the butter, lard, lemon zest, and vanilla. Sift in the cornmeal, flour, baking powder, and a pinch of salt and work them into the mixture.

Drain the raisins, squeeze them gently, and pat dry with paper towels. Mix them into the mixture and let the mixture chill in the refrigerator for at least 1 hour.

Preheat the oven to 350°F/180°C/Gas Mark 4 and line a baking sheet with parchment (baking) paper. Divide the mixture into walnut-size balls, squeezing each one firmly, and space them out on the baking sheet. Bake for about 12–15 minutes. Remove and let cool. Dust with confectioners' (icing) sugar, if using, and serve with zabaglione, if desired.

CIAMBELLINE DI MAIS
CORNMEAL RINGS

AVERAGE

– Preparation time: *45 minutes*
  + 30 minutes chilling time
– Cooking time: *20 minutes*
– Calories per ring: *121*
– *Makes 16*

INGREDIENTS

– 1 cup (6 oz/170 g)
  fine cornmeal
– 3 tablespoons all-purpose
  (plain) flour
– 6 tablespoons (3 oz/85 g)
  butter, softened and cut into
  pieces
– ½ cup (3½ oz/100 g)
  granulated sugar
– 1 egg, beaten
– grated zest of ¼ unwaxed
  lemon
– salt
– confectioners' (icing) sugar,
  for dusting

Sift the cornmeal and flour together into a large bowl, make a well in the center, and add the butter, sugar, and a pinch of salt. Rub the butter quickly but thoroughly into the other ingredients. Stir in the eggs, add the lemon zest, and mix well. Knead gently to achieve a smooth, even dough.

Break off small equal portions of the dough, shape them into cylinders, and join the ends to form a ring. Chill for about 30 minutes or until firm.

Preheat the oven to 350°F/180°C/Gas Mark 4 and line a baking sheet with parchment (baking) paper. Place the dough rings on the baking sheet and bake for about 20 minutes, or until golden. Remove, let cool, and arrange on a platter or large plate. Dust with confectioners' (icing) sugar and serve.

Tip: If you have a kitchen scale, weigh the pieces of dough before shaping them into cylinders to ensure they are consistent in size.

"NZUDDI" BISCOTTI
ALLE MANDORLE
SICILIAN ALMOND COOKIES

EASY

– Preparation time:
  40–50 minutes
– Cooking time: *10 minutes*
– Calories per cookie: *102*
– *Makes 35*

INGREDIENTS

– 1⅔ cups (7 oz/200 g)
  all-purpose (plain) flour
– 1 teaspoon ground
  cinnamon
– 1⅓ cups (7 oz/200 g)
  almonds, roasted and
  chopped
– 1 cup (7 oz/200 g) superfine
  (caster) sugar
– 1 tablespoon finely grated
  orange zest
– 2 eggs
– 2 teaspoons baking powder
– juice of ½ lemon

TO DECORATE

– ½ cup (3½ oz/100 g)
  superfine (caster) sugar
– 3 tablespoons ground
  cinnamon
– ⅔ cup (3½ oz/100 g) shelled
  almonds, roasted and halved

Preheat the oven to 350°F/180°C/Gas Mark 4. Line
1–2 baking sheets with parchment (baking) paper.

Sift the flour and cinnamon into a large bowl, add the
chopped almonds, sugar, and orange zest, and mix well.
Turn out the mixture onto a work surface, make a well
in the middle, and break the eggs into it. Beat lightly
with a fork, then add the baking powder and lemon
juice. Continue to mix with a fork until the mixture
is thick and slightly sticky.

Combine the sugar and cinnamon for decorating
in a shallow bowl and mix well.

Take 1 teaspoon of the cookie (biscuit) dough at a time,
roll into a small ball between the palms of your hands,
then roll it in the sugar and cinnamon mixture. Put the
balls on the prepared baking sheet(s) spaced well apart.
Stick a roasted almond in each ball, pressing down
lightly. Bake for about 10 minutes, until the cookies are
light golden brown. Remove from the oven and transfer
to a wire rack to cool before serving.

LINGUE DOLCI FRIULANE

FRIULI-STYLE COOKIES

AVERAGE

– Preparation time: *45 minutes*
– Cooking time: *25 minutes*
– Calories per cookie: *87*
– *Makes 30*

INGREDIENTS

– ½ cup (3½ oz/100 g) sugar
– 2⅔ cups (12 oz/330 g)
  all-purpose (plain) flour
– 1¼ sticks (5 oz/140 g)
  cold butter
– 1 tablespoon orange-flower
  water
– confectioners' (icing) sugar
– salt

Preheat the oven to 350°F/180°C/Gas Mark 4 and line a baking sheet with parchment (baking) paper.

Make a syrup: pour a scant ½ cup (3½ fl oz/100 ml) water into a small saucepan, add the sugar, and bring to a boil to dissolve the sugar, then cook for 5 minutes and let cool.

To make the dough, combine the flour with the butter and a pinch of salt, mixing the ingredients so that they form a dough that is not smooth but sandy in consistency. Add the sugar syrup and orange-flower water and knead briefly to make a dough.

Take small portions of the dough and shape them into little cylinders, then cut these at an oblique angle into short lengths. Mold them between your palms into long, leaf-shape cookies (biscuits), then make an indentation in each cookie by pressing your thumb into the center.

Place them carefully on the baking sheet and bake for about 20 minutes, or until golden. Remove and let cool to room temperature. Dust with confectioners' (icing) sugar, if using.

BISCOTTI BICOLORI

CHOCOLATE PINWHEEL COOKIES

MODERATE

– Preparation time: *15 minutes,*
  plus 2 hours chilling
– Cooking time: *8–10 minutes*
– Calories per cookie: *114*
– *Makes 24*

INGREDIENTS

– 1¾ sticks (7 oz/200 g)
  butter, softened
– 1 cup (7 oz/200 g) sugar
– 1 egg, beaten
– 2⅔ cups (11 oz/320 g)
  all-purpose (plain) flour
– 1 teaspoon baking powder
– ⅓ cup (1 oz/30 g)
  unsweetened cocoa powder,
  sifted

Cream the butter and sugar in a mixing bowl until soft and fluffy. Beat in the egg, then sift in the flour with the baking powder and fold it in.

Divide the dough in half and carefully mix the cocoa powder into one half. Roll out both doughs ⅛ inch/ 2–3 mm thick on a lightly floured surface and cut them out into 2 rectangles, about 12 x 8 inches/30 x 20 cm. Place one rectangle on top of the other, then roll them up lengthwise. Wrap in plastic wrap (clingfilm) and chill for about 2 hours.

Preheat the oven to 350°F/180°C/Gas Mark 4 and line a baking sheet with parchment (baking) paper.

Cut the rolled dough into slices, ½ inch/1 cm thick. Arrange on the baking sheet and bake for 8–10 minutes. Remove, let cool, and serve.

Tip: To make them easier to slice, after rolling up the dough, wrap the cylinders in plastic wrap and place in the freezer for 30 minutes. Remove the wrap, then cut the dough into disks.

CANESTRELLI PIACENTINI

PIACENZA-STYLE COOKIE

EASY

– Preparation time: *25 minutes*
– Cooking time: *10 minutes*
– Calories per cookie: *102*
– *Makes 35*

INGREDIENTS

– 2 cups (9 oz/250 g)
  all-purpose (plain) flour,
  plus extra for dusting
– 1 egg
– 5 tablespoons (2½ oz/80 g)
  butter, softened and cut into
  small pieces, plus extra for
  greasing
– ⅓ cup (75 g/2½ oz)
  granulated sugar
– grated zest of ¼ unwaxed
  lemon
– ½ teaspoon baking powder
– pinch of apple pie (mixed)
  spice
– few drops of vanilla extract
– 2 tablespoons Alchermes, or
  red food coloring diluted
  with a little rose water
– milk, as needed

Preheat the oven to 350°F/180°C/Gas Mark 4 and grease and dust a baking sheet. Sift the flour into a large bowl, make a well in the center, and break the egg into it. Add the butter, sugar, lemon zest, baking powder, apple pie (mixed) spice, vanilla, and Alchermes and bring together to form a soft dough, adding just enough milk as needed.

Roll out the dough on a lightly floured surface ½ inch/ 1 cm thick and use cookie cutters of various shapes to cut out cookies (biscuits). Place on the baking sheet and bake for about 10 minutes, until slightly browned. Let cool before serving.

Note: The Italian word "canestrelli" is derived from the word "canestri," meaning straw or wicker baskets (canestri) where these cookies were laid to cool after baking.

BISCOTTI DEL CONVENTO

CONVENT COOKIES

– Preparation time: *35 minutes*
– Cooking time: *15 minutes*
– Calories per cookie: *89*
– *Makes 40*

INGREDIENTS

– 4 cups (1 lb 2 oz/500 g)
  all-purpose (plain) flour
– ⅔ cup (4¼ oz/125 g)
  superfine (caster) sugar
– 1 egg plus 1 egg yolk
– 7 tablespoons (3½ oz/100g)
  butter or lard, softened
– ⅓ cup (2 oz/50 g) cream
  of tartar
– pinch of baking soda
  (bicarbonate of soda)
– grated zest of 1 lemon

TO DECORATE

– 1 egg white
– few drops of lemon juice
– ¾ cup (3½ oz/100 g)
  confectioners' (icing) sugar

Preheat the oven to 375°F/190°C/Gas Mark 5. Line a baking sheet with parchment (baking) paper.

Sift the flour into a bowl, make a well in the center, and add the sugar, whole egg, egg yolk, butter, cream of tartar, baking soda (bicarbonate of soda) mixed with a little water, and lemon zest and mix well.

Taking small pieces of dough at a time, make little rolls, then flatten them and cut into diamond shapes. Put them on the prepared baking sheet and bake for about 15 minutes, until light golden brown. Remove from the oven and reduce the oven temperature to 350°F/180°C/Gas Mark 4.

Make the icing. Whisk the egg white with the lemon juice in a bowl, then stir in the icing (confectioners') sugar and mix well. Turn off the oven heat. Dip the cookies (biscuits) in the icing, put them on a baking sheet, and dry them in the oven with the door ajar.

BACI DI DAMA

LADIES' KISSES

– Preparation time: *30 minutes*
– Cooking time: *18–20 minutes*
– Calories per cookie: *124*
– *Makes 25*

INGREDIENTS

– ½ cup (2½ oz/70 g)
  almonds
– 2½ tablespoons superfine
  (caster) sugar
– 7 tablespoons (3½ oz/100 g)
  butter, softened, plus extra
  for greasing
– ¾ cup (3½ oz/100 g)
  all-purpose (plain) flour
– ⅔ cup (3½ oz/100 g) potato
  flour
– generous ½ cup (2½ oz/
  70 g) confectioners' (icing)
  sugar
– 1 egg
– chocolate-hazelnut spread
  (gianduja), to serve

Preheat the oven to 340°F/160°C/Gas Mark 3 and grease a baking sheet. Process the almonds to a powder with superfine (caster) sugar in a food processor. Cream the butter in a bowl, then stir in the flours, confectioners' (icing) sugar, almond and sugar mixture, and the egg, and mix until it forms a smooth dough.

Divide the dough into 50–60 walnut-size balls and flatten them slightly. Arrange on the baking sheet and bake for 18–20 minutes.

Remove from the oven, let cool, then join pairs of the "kisses" together with a little hazelnut-chocolate spread in the middle.

Tip: To enhance the flavor, toast the almonds lightly in the oven until golden brown and let them cool before you blend them with the sugar.

TEGOLE AI PISTACCHI
PISTACHIO WAFERS

EASY

– Preparation time: *30 minutes*
– Cooking time: *8–10 minutes*
– Calories per cookie: *91*
– *Makes 22*

INGREDIENTS

– 7 tablespoons (3½ oz/100 g)
 butter, softened
– ⅓ cup (2 oz/60 g), plus
 1 tablespoon sugar
– few drops of vanilla extract
– 2 egg whites
– ¾ cup (3½ oz/100 g)
 all-purpose (plain)
 flour, sifted
– ⅓ cup (2 oz/50 g) shelled
 pistachios, chopped
– 2½ tablespoons chopped
 pine nuts

Preheat the oven to 350°F/180°C/Gas Mark 4 and line
a baking sheet with parchment (baking) paper. In a bowl,
add the butter, ⅓ cup (2 oz/60 g) sugar, and vanilla
extract and beat until pale and fluffy.

In a clean bowl, whisk the egg whites to stiff peaks. Whisk
in the tablespoon of sugar, then fold this into the butter
and sugar mixture. Sift over the flour and fold in with
the metal spoon.

Use a teaspoon to spoon out small amounts of the dough
onto the baking sheet so that they form irregular circles,
generously spaced apart. Spread thinly with the back of
the spoon. Sprinkle with chopped pistachios and pine
nuts and bake for 8–10 minutes.

While they are still hot, lift them off the sheet, one at a
time, and wrap them halfway around a rolling pin to give
them their characteristic curved shape. Arrange on
a serving dish and let cool before serving.

Note: Tegole, *the Italian word for curved terracotta roof tiles,
are named for their unique shape.*

VENTAGLIETTI AL LIMONE

LEMON PUFF-PASTRY COOKIES

EASY

– Preparation time: *15 minutes*
– Cooking time: *20 minutes*
– Calories per cookie: *109*
– *Makes 15–20*

INGREDIENTS

– 14 oz/400 g ready-to-bake
  puff pastry
– flour, for dusting
– confectioners' (icing) sugar,
  for sprinkling
– 2 unwaxed lemons

Preheat the oven to 350°F/180°C/Gas Mark 4 and line a baking sheet with parchment (baking) paper. Roll out the pastry on a lightly floured surface into a 9-inch/23-cm-wide rectangle, ⅛ inch/3 mm thick, and brush the whole surface with water to dampen it slightly.

Sprinkle the entire surface with sugar and grate the zest of the lemons evenly over it. With one of the short sides nearest you, roll the dough toward the center, starting from both the outside edges at the same time, so that the two cylinders meet in center. Cut across the resulting double cylinder to make ½-inch/1-cm thick slices.

Space out the slices on the baking sheet, pressing them down where the center line was so that the other side fans out as they cook. Bake for 10 minutes, then turn them over and cook for another 10 minutes, until golden brown. Remove, let cool, transfer to a cake plate, and serve.

Tip: Ventaglietti *are the Italian versions of the traditional French* palmiers. *The lemon zest can be replaced with orange and 1 heaping teaspoon ground cinnamon.*

BISCOTTI DEL LAGACCIO

LAGACCIO-STYLE FENNEL COOKIES

AVERAGE

– Preparation time: *1 hour +
1 hour rising and 15 resting time*
– Cooking time: *20 minutes*
– Calories per cookie: *83*
– *Makes 50*

INGREDIENTS

– ⅓ cup (2 oz/50 g) fresh yeast
or ¼ cup (1 oz/25 g) dry
active yeast
– 5¼ cups (1½ lb/650 g)
all-purpose (plain) flour
– 1 stick (4½ oz/125 g)
butter, plus extra for greasing
– 1 cup (7 oz/200 g) sugar
– 2 tablespoons fennel seeds
– salt

Dilute the yeast with a little warm water. Sift 1¼ cups (5 oz/150 g) of the flour into a large bowl, make a well in the center, and add the yeast. Gradually incorporate the flour, adding more lukewarm water as needed to make a soft dough. Shape into a ball, cover, and let rise (proof) in a warm place until it has doubled in volume.

Meanwhile, melt the butter over gentle heat and let cool until just warm. Sift the remaining flour into a mound and make a well in the center, then add a pinch of salt and the melted butter to the well. Add the sugar, fennel seeds and the risen dough. Knead the dough vigorously; its consistency should be fairly soft. Shape it into a ball, dust it with flour, and let rise again in a warm place for an hour until it has doubled in volume.

Preheat the oven to 400°F/200°C/Gas Mark 6 and grease a baking sheet. Punch the dough down, knead it briefly and divide it into 4 equal portions. Shape each portion into a cylinder the size of a very short, thin baguette. Arrange the dough cylinders on it and let stand in a warm place for about 15 minutes.

Slice the cylinders into pieces ½ inch/1 cm thick and place them on the baking sheet. Bake for 20 minutes or until pale golden brown, then remove and let cool. Store in an airtight glass container.

Note: The name of this biscuit originates from a famous district in Genoa called quartiere del lagaccio.

CANTUCCINI
ALMOND AND PINE NUT CANTUCCINI

EASY

- Preparation time: *30 minutes*
- Cooking time:
  1 hour 8 minutes
- Calories per serving: *420*
- *Serves 8*

INGREDIENTS

- melted butter, for greasing
- ⅔ cup (3½ oz/100 g)
  unskinned almonds
- ⅓ cup (1½ oz/40 g)
  pine nuts
- generous 2 cups (9 oz/250 g)
  all-purpose (plain) flour
- 1¾ cups (7½ oz/220 g)
  confectioners' (icing) sugar
- 1 teaspoon baking powder
- 2 eggs

Preheat the oven to 400°F/200°C/Gas Mark 6 and grease a baking sheet. Put the almonds and pine nuts onto the baking sheet and lightly toast them in the oven for 5 minutes. Remove, let cool, and split the almonds in half.

Sift the flour, sugar, and baking powder into a large bowl, make a well in the center, break the eggs into it, and gradually mix them into the dry ingredients. Add the pine nuts and almonds. When the dough is smooth, divide it in half and shape it into 2 cylinders about 12 inches/30 cm long.

Place them on the baking sheet and bake for about 18 minutes. Remove, let cool a little, and reduce the oven temperature to 270°F/130°C/Gas Mark 1. Cut the cylinders into diagonal ½-inch/1-cm-thick slices. Return the slices to the baking sheet and bake for 45 minutes.

Remove from the oven, let cool completely, and store in an airtight container lined with wax (greaseproof) paper. Serve with ice cream or sweet wine.

CANTUCCINI AL CAFFÈ

COFFEE AND ALMOND CANTUCCINI

EASY

– Preparation time: *30 minutes*
– Cooking time: *20 minutes*
– Calories per cookie: *83*
– *Makes 32*

INGREDIENTS

– butter, for greasing
– 3¼ cups (14 oz/400 g)
  all-purpose (plain) flour
– 1½ teaspoons baking
  powder
– 4 eggs
– ½ cup (3½ oz/100 g)
  acacia honey
– 5 teaspoons strong
  black coffee
– few drops of vanilla extract
– ⅔ cup (3½ oz/100 g)
  unskinned almonds

Preheat the oven to 400°F/200°C/Gas Mark 6 and grease a baking sheet. Sift the flour and baking powder into in a large bowl and make a well in the center. Break the eggs into it and add the honey, coffee, vanilla, and almonds. Combine all the ingredients to form a dough.

Shape the dough into cylinders, 1¼ inch/3 cm in diameter, flatten them slightly, and arrange on the baking sheet. Bake for 20 minutes, until golden brown. Cut into lozenge-shape slices while still hot. Let cool before serving.

Tip: For even crisper cookies (biscuits), after cutting the slices, toast them lightly in the oven, turning them once.

CAKES

STEP 1

STEP 2

STEP 3

STEP 4

CIAMBELLA ALL'ARANCIA

ORANGE CAKE

EASY

– Preparation time: *15 minutes*
– Cooking time: *30 minutes*
– Calories per serving: *692*
– *Serves 6*

INGREDIENTS

– 1 stick plus 1 tablespoon
  (4½ oz/130 g) softened
  butter, plus extra for
  greasing
– 1 cup (7 oz/200 g) sugar
– 3 eggs, beaten
– 2⅓ cups (10 oz/300 g)
  all-purpose (plain) flour
– 2 teaspoons baking powder
– juice of 3 oranges, strained
– 1 teaspoon grated orange
  zest

STEP 1

Preheat the oven to 350°F/180°C/Gas Mark 4, grease
a 9½-inch/24-cm tube pan (ring mold), and put it into
the refrigerator. In a large bowl, beat the butter and
sugar until light and creamy. Beat in the eggs gradually.

STEP 2

Sift the flour and baking powder into a bowl.

STEP 3

Fold the flour mixture into the butter and sugar mixture,
then mix in half of the orange juice and all
of the orange zest.

STEP 4

Pour the cake batter into the pan and bake for about
30 minutes. Remove, let cool a little, and turn the cake
out onto a serving dish. Prick it all over with a toothpick
(cocktail stick), then moisten the cake by pouring
teaspoons of the remaining orange juice into the holes.
Let cool, then serve.

EASY CAKE

EASY

- Preparation time: *25 minutes*
- Cooking time: *35–40 minutes*
- Calories per serving: *439*
- *Serves 6*

INGREDIENTS

- 7 tablespoons (3½ oz/100 g) butter, softened, plus extra for greasing
- flour, for dusting
- 1 cup (7 oz/200 g) sugar
- 3 eggs, separated
- 1⅔ cups (9 oz/250 g) potato flour
- 2 teaspoons baking powder
- 2 teaspoons vanilla sugar (see page 31)
- warm milk, as needed
- salt

Preheat the oven to 325°F/160°C/Gas Mark 3 and grease and dust a 6-cup (50-fl oz/1.5-liter) tube pan (ring mold). In a large bowl, beat the butter and all but 2 tablespoons of the sugar until light and fluffy. Add a pinch of salt. Beat in the 3 egg yolks.

In a separate bowl, sift the flour and baking powder. Mix the dry ingredients into the butter and egg mixture, stirring continuously. Add a little milk to achieve a soft dropping consistency and stir well. Whisk the egg whites to stiff peaks, add the remaining 2 tablespoons sugar. Fold into the flour mixture.

Pour the cake batter into the pan—it should only be filled halfway. Bake for 35–40 minutes. Let stand in the pan for 5 minutes, then turn out onto a wire rack to cool completely. Dust with the vanilla sugar before serving.

TORTINI AI CANDITI

CANDIED FRUIT CUPCAKES

EASY

– Preparation time: *15 minutes*
– Cooking time: *18–20 minutes*
– Calories per serving: *513*
– *Serves 6*

INGREDIENTS

– scant 1 cup (4¼ oz/125 g)
  all-purpose (plain) flour
– 1½ teaspoons baking
  powder
– 7 tablespoons (3½ oz/100 g)
  butter, plus extra, melted,
  for greasing
– ½ cup (3½ oz/100 g) sugar
– 2 eggs
– 1 tablespoon kirsch or
  maraschino
– 1 heaping tablespoon
  coarsely chopped candied
  (mixed) peel or candied
  (glacé) cherries
– confectioners' (icing) sugar,
  for dusting

Preheat the oven to 375°F/190°C/Gas Mark 5 and line
a 6-cup muffin pan with paper liners (cases).

Sift the flour and baking powder together. Beat the butter
and sugar until light and fluffy, then add the eggs one
at a time, alternating with the flour mixture. Add the kirsch
or maraschino and continue mixing for about 1 minute.
Stir in the candied (mixed) peel or candied (glacé)
cherries. Mix until thoroughly combined.

Place equal amounts of batter in each liner, filling
them halfway. Bake for 18–20 minutes. Remove, let cool,
and place on a serving dish. Dust with confectioners'
(icing) sugar to serve.

TORTA DEL DONIZETTI

DONIZETTI'S CAKE

EASY

– Preparation time: *30 minutes*
– Cooking time: *40 minutes*
– Calories per serving: *262–294*
– *Serves 6–8*

INGREDIENTS

– 1¼ sticks plus 2 tablespoons
  (5½ oz/160 g) butter,
  softened, plus extra for
  greasing
– generous ⅓ cup (3 oz/85 g)
  superfine (caster) sugar
– 4 egg yolks
– 2 egg whites
– 1 tablespoon lemon juice
– 3 tablespoons (1 oz/25 g)
  all-purpose (plain) flour,
  sifted
– ½ cup (2½ oz/60 g) potato
  starch or cornstarch
  (cornflour), sifted
– ½ teaspoon baking powder
– ⅓ cup (2 oz/50 g) dried
  apricots
– 2 tablespoons maraschino
  liqueur, to taste
– few drops of vanilla extract
– confectioners' (icing) sugar,
  for dusting

Preheat the oven to 350°F/180°C/Gas Mark 4 and grease a 9½-inch/24-cm tube pan (ring mold). Beat the butter in a bowl with half the sugar, then stir in the egg yolks and mix thoroughly.

Whisk the egg whites with the lemon juice to stiff peaks, then whisk in the remaining sugar, and fold into the butter mixture. Gradually fold in the flour and potato starch, baking powder, apricots, maraschino liqueur, and vanilla. Turn the batter into the pan. Bake for about 40 minutes.

Remove, turn out, and let cool before dusting the cake with confectioners' (icing) sugar to serve.

TORTINE AL PROFUMO DI LIMONE

MINI LEMON LOAF CAKES

– Preparation time: *15 minutes*
– Cooking time*: 18–20 minutes*
– Calories per serving: *232*
– *Makes 6–8*

INGREDIENTS

– 7 tablespoons (3½ oz/100 g)
  butter, plus extra for greasing
– scant 1 cup (4¼ oz/125 g)
  all-purpose (plain) flour
– 1½ teaspoons baking powder
– ½ cup (3½ oz/100 g) sugar
– 2 eggs
– 1 tablespoon lemon juice
– grated zest of ½ lemon
– 1 tablespoon lemon liqueur
  (optional)
– confectioners' (icing) sugar,
  to serve

Preheat the oven to 375°F/190°C/Gas Mark 5 and grease the sections of a mini loaf pan.

Sift the flour and baking powder into a large bowl. In a separate bowl, beat the butter and sugar together until light and creamy. Add the eggs one at a time, then stir in the flour mixture and lemon zest, alternating with the lemon juice. Place an equal amount of the batter in each section and bake for 18–20 minutes.

Remove from the oven and let cool, then remove from the pan and dust with confectioners' (icing) sugar. Serve.

Tip: These lemon cakes can be made richer by adding scant ½ cup (2¼ oz/80 g) of white chocolate chips to the mixture.

EASY

- Preparation time: *10 minutes*
- Cooking time: *25 minutes*
- Calories per serving: *315*
- *Makes 12*

INGREDIENTS

- butter, for greasing
- 5 oz/150 g milk caramels
- ⅓ cup (5 oz/50 g) blanched almonds
- 1⅔ cups (7 oz/200 g) all-purpose (plain) flour
- ½ cup (3½ oz/100 g) granulated sugar
- ⅓ cup (3 fl oz/80 ml) mild olive or sunflower oil
- 4 tablespoons unsweetened cocoa powder
- 2 eggs, beaten
- generous 1 cup (9 oz/250 g) vanilla yogurt
- 2 teaspoons baking powder

Preheat the oven to 350°F/180°C/Gas Mark 4 and grease a muffin pan or 12 individual cake molds. Put all the ingredients into a blender or food processor and process at medium speed until evenly mixed.

Divide the batter equally among the muffin pan or cake molds and bake for 25 minutes. Serve warm.

Tip: The vanilla yogurt can be substituted with plain (natural) yogurt and ½ teaspoon vanilla extract.

CIAMBELLA AL LIMONE

LEMON CAKE

EASY

– Preparation time: *20 minutes,*
  plus 15 minutes rising time
– Cooking time: *40 minutes*
– Calories per serving: *244*
– *Serves 6*

INGREDIENTS

– 2 cups (9 oz/250 g)
  all-purpose (plain) flour
– 1½ tablespoons active dry
  yeast
– 2 tablespoons sugar
– 1 cup (8 fl oz/250 ml) milk,
  warmed
– generous ½ cup (2¾ oz/80 g)
  golden raisins (sultanas)
– 1 egg, lightly beaten
– grated zest of 1 unwaxed
  lemon
– salt

Preheat the oven to 400°F/200°C/Gas Mark 6 and grease a 9½-inch/24-cm tube pan (ring mold). Combine the flour, yeast, and sugar in a bowl with a little lukewarm milk. Let rise in a warm place for 15 minutes. Meanwhile, soak the golden raisins (sultanas) in warm water.

Squeeze the raisins dry and add to the dough along with the remaining milk, egg, lemon zest, and a pinch of salt. Knead the dough, shape it into a tube, and place in the pan. Make shallow, angled incisions along the surface, and bake for 40 minutes. Let cool and serve.

CIAMBELLA ALLE CAROTE

CARROT CAKE

EASY

- Preparation time: *20 minutes*
- Cooking time: *45 minutes*
- Calories per serving: *316*
- *Serves 6*

INGREDIENTS

- 1 cup plus 2 tablespoons
  (5 oz/140 g) all-purpose
  (plain) flour, for dusting
- ¾ cup (5 oz/150 g) sugar
- 1 teaspoon baking powder
- pinch of ground ginger
- pinch of ground nutmeg
- 2 tablespoons milk
- scant ½ cup (3½ fl oz/
  100 ml) olive oil
- 2½ tablespoons (30 g/
  1¼ oz) butter, melted, plus
  extra for greasing
- 2 eggs
- ⅓ cup (2 oz/50 g) small
  raisins or currants
- ¼ cup (¾ oz/20 g) chopped
  walnuts
- 2 carrots, peeled and grated
- confectioners' (icing) sugar,
  for dusting
- salt

Preheat the oven to 325°F/160°C/Gas Mark 3 and grease and dust a 6-cup tube pan (ring mold). Mix the flour, sugar, baking powder, ginger, nutmeg, and a pinch of salt in a large bowl.

Add the milk, oil, butter, and eggs. Mix until well blended, then work in the raisins or currants and walnuts until well distributed. Finally, add the grated carrots.

Transfer the batter to the pan and bake for about 45 minutes. Remove and let cool completely. Turn out onto a serving dish, dust liberally with confectioners' (icing) sugar, and serve in slices.

Tip: To dust a tube pan after you have greased it, sprinkle it liberally with flour, dusting it all over the inside, then turn it upside down and tap it to get rid of the excess flour.

CIAMBELLINE AL LIMONE

LITTLE LEMON RINGS

EASY

– Preparation time: *20 minutes*
– Cooking time: *20–25 minutes*
– Calories per serving: *645–484*
– *Serves 6–8*

INGREDIENTS

– 1¾ sticks (7 oz/200 g) butter, softened, plus extra for greasing
– 1 cup (7 oz/200 g) sugar
– 2¾ cups (12 oz/350 g) all-purpose (plain) flour
– 2½ teaspoons baking powder
– 3 eggs
– 2 lemons
– 2 tablespoons milk
– 3–4 tablespoons confectioners' (icing) sugar
– salt

Preheat the oven to 350°F/180°C/Gas Mark 4 and grease 6–8 mini Bundt pans. Using a wire balloon whisk, beat the butter and sugar in a bowl until pale and fluffy. Sift the flour with the baking powder in a separate bowl. Stir in one egg at a time, alternating with the flour mixture, then add the juice of 1 lemon, the grated zest of ½ lemon, milk, and a pinch of salt.

Stir until the mixture is well blended. Place an equal amount of batter in each pan. Bake for 20–25 minutes.

Meanwhile, cut off strips of zest from the remaining lemon and squeeze the juice. Pour the juice into a small saucepan, add a scant ½ cup (3½ fl oz/100 ml) water and the confectioners' (icing) sugar. Place over medium heat and bring to a boil to make a fairly thin icing of pouring consistency.

As soon as the cakes are cooked, remove and let cool, then turn them out and pour a thin coating of the lemon icing over them. Decorate with the strips of lemon zest.

CIAMBELLONE MARMORIZZATO

MARBLED CAKE

AVERAGE

– Preparation time: *30 minutes*
– Cooking time: *30–35 minutes*
– Calories per serving: *643*
– *Serves 8*

INGREDIENTS

– 2¾ sticks (11 oz/300 g) butter, softened, plus extra for greasing
– 1½ cups (11 oz/300 g) sugar
– 5 eggs, separated
– 3 cups (12 oz/350 g) all-purpose (plain) flour
– 1 tablespoon baking powder
– grated zest of 1 unwaxed lemon
– juice of ½ lemon
– 2 tablespoons unsweetened cocoa powder
– 2 tablespoons milk
– confectioners' (icing) sugar, for dusting
– salt

Preheat the oven to 350°F/180°C/Gas Mark 4 and grease and flour a 10-inch/25-cm tube pan (ring mold). Beat the butter and sugar until light and creamy. Add the eggs, one at a time, to the batter, beating well between each one. Sift the flour and baking powder and fold into the batter until combined.

Divide the batter in half. Stir the lemon zest and juice into one half and the unsweetened cocoa powder and milk into the other. Fill the pan with the cake batter, alternating spoonfuls of the chocolate batter with the lemon batter. Push a toothpick (cocktail stick) into the surface of the batter and trace lines to blur the colors. Tap the bottom of the pan on the work surface and bake for 30–35 minutes, or until a toothpick or skewer is inserted and comes out clean. Remove from the oven and let cool before unmolding. Dust with confectioners' (icing) sugar.

Tip: To soften butter quickly, wash and dry your hands and work it by hand, which will warm and soften it at the same time.

TORTA DI ALBICOCCHE

APRICOT CAKE

EASY

– Preparation time: *35 minutes*
– Cooking time: *1 hour*
– Calories per serving: *509*
– *Serves 8*

INGREDIENTS

– 1¾ lb/800 g apricots
– 2 sticks (8 oz/225 g)
  butter
– 1¼ cups (9 oz/250 g)
  superfine sugar
– 4 eggs, lightly beaten
– 3¾ cups (1 lb 1 oz/475 g)
  all-purpose (plain) flour
– 2 teaspoons baking powder
– ⅓ cup (1½ oz/40 g)
  chopped pistachio nuts

Preheat the oven to 375°F/190°C/Gas Mark 5. Line a 9-inch/23-cm cake pan with parchment (baking) paper. Put the apricots into a bowl, pour in boiling water to cover, and let stand for 15 seconds, then drain. Peel off the skins, halve, and remove the pits, then cut each half into 2 pieces.

Beat together the butter and sugar in a bowl until creamy, then fold in the eggs, one at a time. Sift the flour and baking powder over the mixture and stir in, then stir in the apricots.

Pour the batter into the prepared pan, sprinkle with the pistachios, and bake for about 1 hour, until risen and golden. Let stand in the pan for 5 minutes, then transfer to a wire rack to cool.

TORTA CAPOVOLTA DI BANANE

UPSIDE-DOWN BANANA CAKE

EASY

– Preparation time: *25 minutes*
– Cooking time: *40 minutes*
– Calories per serving: *371*
– *Serves 8*

INGREDIENTS

– 4 tablespoons (2 oz/60 g)
  butter, plus extra for
  greasing
– 5 bananas
– 1 tablespoon packed brown
  sugar
– ⅓ cup (2½ fl oz/75 ml)
  Grand Marnier
– 5 oz/150 g semisweet (dark)
  chocolate
– confectioners' (icing) sugar,
  for dusting
– ½ quantity Basic Pie Dough
  (Shortcrust Pastry), see
  page 105

Preheat the oven to 400°F/200°C/Gas Mark 6 and grease a round 8-inch/20-cm baking pan. Peel the bananas and cut them in half lengthwise. Melt half the butter with the brown sugar in a skillet or frying pan over medium heat and add the halved bananas. Cook until golden, sprinkle with the liqueur and let this evaporate. Remove from the heat and set aside.

Melt the chocolate in a heatproof bowl set over a saucepan of barely simmering water and, stirring continuously, add the remaining butter. Dust the baking pan with confectioners' (icing) sugar and arrange the halved bananas inside in a flower shape, radiating from the center. Drizzle the melted chocolate over the bananas, reserving a tablespoon to decorate.

Roll out the dough on a lightly floured surface into a disk at least ¾ inch/2 cm larger in diameter than the baking pan and cover the bananas with it. Tuck the edges down inside the baking pan to enclose the bananas. Bake for about 30 minutes.

Remove and let rest for 5 minutes, then turn out upside down onto a serving dish. Decorate with the reserved melted chocolate and serve hot or warm.

Tip: Be careful when pouring the chocolate onto the bananas, making sure that it does not ooze into the bottom of the baking pan, where it tends to burn in the intense heat of the oven.

PLUM-CAKE ALLE NOCCIOLE

CHOCOLATE AND HAZELNUT LOAF

EASY

– Preparation time: *20 minutes*
– Cooking time: *40 minutes*
– Calories per serving: *376*
– *Serves 4*

INGREDIENTS

– ¾ cup (3½ oz/100 g)
  hazelnuts
– 6 egg whites
– ¾ cup (5 oz/150 g) sugar
– ½ cup (2 oz/50 g)
  unsweetened cocoa powder,
  sifted
– confectioners' (icing) sugar,
  for dusting
– salt

Preheat the oven to 350°F/180°C/Gas Mark 4 and line a loaf pan with parchment (baking) paper. Toast the hazelnuts in the oven, then remove their skins by rubbing them with a clean, coarse dish towel and let cool. Reduce the oven temperature to 275°F/140°C/Gas Mark 1.

In a large bowl, whisk the egg whites with a pinch of salt to stiff peaks, then whisk in the sugar a little at a time.

Chop the hazelnuts finely and fold them into the egg white mixture with the cocoa powder. Stir gently. Turn the batter into the loaf pan and bake for 40 minutes. Remove and let cool to lukewarm, then turn the cake out onto a serving dish. Dust with confectioners' (icing) sugar, cut into slices, and serve.

TORTINE ALLA CREMA
DI CIOCCOLATO
CHOCOLATE CUSTARD CUPCAKES

EASY

– Preparation time: *15 minutes*
– Cooking time: *25 minutes*
– Calories per serving: *277*
– *Makes 12*

INGREDIENTS

– 1 cup (3½ oz/100 g) skinned almonds, finely chopped
– 1⅔ cups (7 oz/200 g) all-purpose (plain) flour
– 1½ teaspoons baking powder
– generous 1 cup (9 oz/250 g) full-fat plain yogurt
– 6 tablespoons oil
– ½ cup (3½ oz/100 g) sugar
– 2 eggs
– few drops of vanilla extract
– ⅓ cup (3½ oz/100 g) prepared thick chocolate custard or chocolate pudding

Preheat the oven to 350°F/180°C/Gas Mark 4 and line a 12-cup muffin pan with paper liners (cases).

Put the almonds into a bowl with the flour and baking powder. Add the yogurt, oil, sugar, eggs, and vanilla extract and mix until well combined.

Spoon a little batter into each liner, followed by a generous teaspoon of chocolate custard, and cover with a layer of cake batter until three-quarters full. Bake for 25 minutes. Remove and let cool before serving.

CIAMBELLA AL CIOCCOLATO

MOCHA CAKE WITH RUM

– Preparation time: *20 minutes*
– Cooking time: *40 minutes*
– Calories per serving: *587–470*
– *Serves 8–10*

INGREDIENTS

– 1¾ cups plus 2 tablespoons
  (13 oz/370 g) sugar
– 1⅓ cups (7 oz/200 g)
  all-purpose (plain) flour
– 1½ teaspoons baking powder
– 4 tablespoons unsweetened
  cocoa powder, plus extra for
  dusting
– 4 tablespoons instant coffee
– 1 teaspoon baking soda
  (bicarbonate of soda)
– 1¼ cups (10 fl oz/300 ml) oil
– ½ cup (4¼ oz/125 g) plain
  yogurt
– 3 tablespoons rum
– 3 eggs
– confectioners' (icing) sugar,
  for dusting
– salt

Preheat the oven to 400°F/200°C/Gas Mark 6 and grease and dust a Bundt pan. Place the sugar, flour, baking powder, cocoa powder, coffee, baking soda (bicarbonate of soda), and a pinch of salt in the bowl of the food processor and process. Add the oil, yogurt, and rum. Process, then add the eggs, one at a time, and process until well mixed. Pour it into the pan.

Bake for 40 minutes. Let cool completely, then turn out the cake. Dust with cocoa powder and confectioners' (icing) sugar, cut into slices, and serve.

PLUM-CAKE DI RISO

FRUIT, NUT, AND CHOCOLATE LOAF

INGREDIENTS

– flour, for dusting
– ½ cup (2¾ oz/80 g)
  golden raisins (sultanas)
– 2 tablespoons rum
– 2 cups (18 fl oz/500 ml) milk
– scant 1 cup (5 oz/150 g)
  short-grain pudding rice
– 4 tablespoons (2 oz/50 g)
  butter, softened and cut
  into small pieces, plus extra
  for greasing
– 3 eggs, separated
– ½ cup (3½ oz/100 g) sugar
– ⅓ cup (1½ oz/40 g)
  skinned walnuts, finely
  chopped
– 2 oz/50 g semisweet (dark)
  chocolate, finely chopped
– 1½ oz/40 g candied (glacé)
  peel, finely chopped
– salt

Preheat the oven to 350°F/180°C/Gas Mark 4, grease and dust a loaf pan. Rinse the golden raisins (sultanas) and soak them in the rum in a small bowl.

Place the milk and rice in a heavy saucepan, heat slowly to boiling point over medium-low heat and cook for about 30 minutes. Remove from the heat and let cool to lukewarm. Process in a blender until smooth.

Pour the rice mixture into a bowl and add the butter, egg yolks, and sugar. Stir in the walnuts, chocolate, candied peel, and soaked sultanas and stir well.

In a separate bowl, whisk the egg whites with a pinch of salt to stiff peaks and fold into the cake batter.

Spoon the batter into the pan. Tap the bottom on a work surface to get rid of any air pockets and bake for 1 hour. Let cool, turn out, and serve.

TORTINI CON ANICE
E PINOLI

ANISEED AND PINE NUT CUPCAKES

INGREDIENTS

– butter, for greasing
– 2 cups (9 oz/250 g)
  all-purpose (plain) flour
– 1 teaspoon baking
  powder
– 3 teaspoons ground aniseed
– ¾ cup (3½ oz/100 g) pine
  nuts, chopped
– 2 eggs, lightly beaten
– ½ cup (3½ oz/100 g) sugar
– ⅓ cup (3 fl oz/80 ml)
  vegetable oil
– 1¼ cups (11 fl oz/300 ml)
  milk
– juice of 1 lemon, strained
– 2 tablespoons confectioners'
  (icing) sugar

Preheat the oven to 350°F/180°C/Gas Mark 4 and grease a 12-cup muffin pan. Sift the flour into a bowl with the baking powder, sprinkle in 2 teaspoons aniseed and the pine nuts, then stir in the eggs, sugar, oil, and milk. Pour the batter into the pan and bake for 20 minutes.

Meanwhile, make the icing. In a bowl, combine the lemon juice, 1 teaspoon aniseed, and the confectioners' (icing) sugar and mix until thoroughly combined.

Remove the cakes, let cool until just warm, and brush them with the lemon icing. Serve.

Tip: To grind the aniseeds, you can crush them in a mortar with a pestle or grind them in a spice grinder with 1 tablespoon sugar.

TARTS

PASTA FROLLA CLASSICA
BASIC PIE DOUGH (SHORTCRUST PASTRY)

EASY

- Preparation time: *5 minutes +
  30 minutes chilling*
- Cooking time: *varies with
  recipe*
- Calories per serving: *330*
- *Makes 1 lb/450 g*

INGREDIENTS

- 2⅓ cups (11 oz/300 g)
  all-purpose (plain) flour
- 1 vanilla bean
- ⅓ cup plus 1 tablespoon
  (3 oz/80 g) sugar
- 1¼ sticks (5 oz/150 g) cold
  butter
- 1 egg plus 2 egg yolks
- salt

STEP 1

Put the flour into the food processor. Slit the vanilla bean lengthwise, scrape out the seeds with a small knife, and add them to the flour together with the sugar, a pinch of salt, and the butter. (For a chocolate pie dough, add ½ cup (2 oz/50 g) unsweetened cocoa powder, sifted, with the sugar.)

STEP 2

Process in a food processor until the mixture resembles bread crumbs, add the egg and egg yolks, and turn off the food processor as soon as a dough ball is formed.

STEP 3

Wrap the dough in plastic wrap (clingfilm) and rest it in the refrigerator for at least 30 minutes.

STEP 4

Use the dough as needed in your recipe.

Tip: Add the diced cold butter straight from the refrigerator and as soon as the ingredients cohere, stop mixing. Always rest the dough for the time indicated. The dough can be stored in the freezer.

CROSTATA DI FRUTTA

FRUIT TART

AVERAGE

– Preparation time: *25 minutes*
– Cooking time: *30 minutes*
– Calories per serving: *540*
– *Serves 8*

INGREDIENTS

– ½ quantity Basic Pie Dough
  (Shortcrust Pastry), see
  page 105
– flour, for dusting
– 2½ teaspoons powdered
  gelatin
– 1¼ cups (11 fl oz/300 ml)
  heavy (double) or whipping
  cream
– scant ½ cup (3½ oz/100 g)
  lemon curd
– confectioners' (icing) sugar,
  for dusting
– 1 banana
– juice of ½ lemon
– 2 kiwi
– 1¼ cups (6 oz/150 g)
  strawberries
– 1 cup (5 oz/175 g)
  raspberries

Preheat the oven to 400°F/200°C/Gas Mark 6 and grease an 8½-inch/22-cm baking pan. Roll out the basic pie dough (shortcrust pastry) on a lightly floured surface to a disk about ⅛ inch/3 mm thick and use it to line the pan. Rinse and squeeze dry a sheet of parchment (baking) paper, prick the pastry bottom with a fork, cover it with the parchment paper, and fill with pie weights (baking beans).

Bake for 20 minutes. Remove the parchment paper and pie weights and cook for another 5 minutes. Let cool and transfer to a cooling rack.

Soak the gelatin in ¼ cup (2 fl oz/50 ml) of cold water for a few minutes. Whip the cream in a bowl to soft peaks and put aside. Melt the gelatin in a small saucepan over low heat, then stir it into the lemon curd and add half the whipped cream. Stirring gently with a figure-eight movement, add the remaining cream. Pour this filling into the pastry shell (case) and spread it out evenly with a spoon.

Prepare the fruit: Slice the banana and coat in the lemon juice. Peel and thinly slice the kiwi. Trim and quarter the strawberries. Decorate the tart with the fruit, dust with confectioners' (icing) sugar, and serve.

Tip: You can coat the fruit with a little preserves instead of dusting it with confectioners' sugar. Put a heaping tablespoon of apricot preserves into a small saucepan, add 2 tablespoons of orange or lemon juice or water, melt it over a low heat, and brush it over the fruit.

TARTELETTE AL LIMONE E KIWI
LEMON AND KIWI TARTLETS

EASY

– Preparation time: *20 minutes*
– Cooking time: *10–12 minutes*
– Calories per serving: *317*
– *Serves 6*

INGREDIENTS

– butter, for greasing
– flour, for dusting
– ⅓ quantity Basic Pie Dough (Shortcrust Pastry), see page 105
– 1 cup (8 fl oz/250 ml) milk
– 3 egg yolks
– ⅔ cup (4½ oz/125 g) sugar
– 3 tablespoons potato flour
– 2 lemons
– 2 ripe kiwi, sliced

Preheat the oven to 350°F/180°C/Gas Mark 4 and grease and dust 6 fluted tartlet molds. Divide the basic pie dough (shortcrust pastry) into 6 equal pieces. Roll them out on a lightly floured surface, not too thinly, and use them to line the tartlet molds. Bake for 10–12 minutes.

Meanwhile, pour the milk into a small saucepan and bring to a boil, then remove the pan from the heat. In another bowl, use a hand blender to whisk the egg yolks with the sugar, then add the potato flour and the grated zest of 1 lemon. Keep whisking while pouring in the hot milk in a thin stream. Return to the pan and cook over low heat, stirring constantly, until thickened.

Remove from the heat and continue stirring while adding the juice of both lemons. Let cool, then spoon the lemon custard into the tartlets. Decorate with kiwi fruit slices and serve.

CROSTATA DI PASTA FROLLA CON RICOTTA E LAMPONI

RICOTTA AND RASPBERRY TART

EASY

– Preparation time: *25 minutes*
– Cooking time: *45 minutes*
– Calories per serving: *582*
– *Serves 8*

INGREDIENTS

– butter, for greasing
– flour, for dusting
– ⅔ quantity Basic Pie Dough
  (Shortcrust Pastry), see
  page 105
– 2½ cups (1¼ lb/600 g)
  ricotta cheese
– 1 egg plus 2 egg yolks
– 1 cup (7 oz/200 g) sugar
– 2½ cups (11 oz/300 g)
  raspberries
– confectioners' (icing) sugar,
  for dusting
– salt

Preheat the oven to 350°F/180°C/Gas Mark 4 and grease and dust a 10-inch/25-cm fluted tart pan. Roll out the basic pie dough (shortcrust pastry) on a lightly floured surface and use it to line the baking pan.

Cream the ricotta cheese in a bowl, then add the egg, followed by the egg yolks one at a time, the sugar, and a pinch of salt. Spoon the filling into the pastry shell (case), smoothing it out without squashing it. Bake for 45 minutes. Remove from the oven and let cool, then put the raspberries on top. Dust with confectioners' (icing) sugar and serve warm.

Tip: To transfer the pie dough into a baking pan easily, roll it out directly onto parchment (baking) paper, then use both to line the baking pan.

CROSTATA ALL'ARANCIA

ORANGE TART

EASY

– Preparation time: *15 minutes*
 + 30 minutes resting
– Cooking time: *30 minutes*
– Calories per serving: *453*
– *Serves 8*

INGREDIENTS

– ⅔ quantity Basic Pie Dough
 (Shortcrust Pastry), see
 page 105
– flour, for dusting
– 1 cup (3½ oz/100 g) slivered
 (flaked) almonds
– 2 eggs
– ½ cup (3½ oz/100 g) sugar
– grated zest of 1 and juice
 of 2 unwaxed oranges,
 strained, plus 1 whole
 unwaxed orange
– 4 tablespoons (2½ oz/60 g)
 butter, melted
– confectioners' (icing) sugar
 for dusting

Preheat the oven to 375°F/190°C/Gas Mark 5 and line
a 10-inch/25-cm round fluted tart pan with parchment
(baking) paper. Roll out the basic pie dough (shortcrust
pastry) into a disk on a lightly floured surface, line the
bottom and sides of the baking pan with it and sprinkle
the slivered (flaked) almonds over the bottom.

Beat the eggs and the sugar in a large heatproof bowl until
pale and fluffy, add the orange zest and juice. Place the
bowl over a large saucepan of simmering water and whisk
until the mixture has increased in volume and thickened
enough to coat the back of a spoon. Remove from the heat
and stir in the melted butter.

Let the filling cool. Cut the remaining, unpeeled, orange
into wafer-thin disks, dust with confectioners' sugar, and set
aside. Spoon the filling into the pastry shell (case), smooth
it level and cover with the orange slices. Bake for
25 minutes. Remove from the oven, let rest for a few
minutes, then transfer the tart to a serving dish.

CROSTATA AI FRUTTI DI BOSCO

MIXED BERRY TART

EASY

– Preparation time: *15 minutes*
  + 30 minutes resting
– Cooking time: *10–15 minutes*
– Calories per serving: *298*
– *Serves 8*

INGREDIENTS

– 1½ cups (6 oz/175 g)
  raspberries
– 1 cup (5 oz/150 g)
  blackberries
– 1 cup (4 oz/120 g)
  strawberries, hulled and
  sliced
– ⅔ quantity Basic Pie Dough
  (Shortcrust Pastry), see
  page 105
– flour, for dusting
– ⅓ cup (3½ oz/100 g)
  blueberry preserves (jam)
– confectioners' (icing) sugar,
  for dusting

Preheat the oven to 350°F/180°C/Gas Mark 4 and line a 10-inch/25-cm round baking pan with parchment (baking) paper. Rinse the berries and dry them on paper towels.

Roll out the basic pie dough (shortcrust pastry) into a disk on a lightly floured surface and use it to line the bottom and sides of the baking pan. Cover with parchment paper that has been moistened and squeezed dry, add the pie weights (baking beans) and bake for 10–15 minutes. Remove and discard the parchment paper and weights. Transfer the pastry shell (case) to a serving dish and spread a thin layer of blueberry preserves (jam) over the bottom.

Arrange the blackberries in 3 vertical rows on the preserves, the raspberries in 3 horizontal rows, and the strawberries in the gaps. Dust the tart with sifted confectioners' (icing) sugar and serve.

CROSTATA D'ALBICOCCHE

APRICOT TART

EASY

– Preparation time: *10 minutes*
– Cooking time: *20–25 minutes*
– Calories per serving: *317*
– *Serves 6*

INGREDIENTS

– 10 canned or bottled apricot
  halves in syrup
– ⅔ quantity Basic Pie Dough
  (Shortcrust Pastry), see
  page 105
– flour, for dusting
– 4 ladyfingers (sponge
  fingers)
– ⅓ cup (3½ oz/100 g) apricot
  preserves (jam)

Preheat the oven to 350°F/180°C/Gas Mark 4 and line a 10-inch/25-cm round baking pan with parchment (baking) paper. Meanwhile, drain the apricot halves of their syrup and set aside to finish draining in a colander.

Roll out the basic pie dough (shortcrust pastry) into a disk on a lightly floured surface, and fit it snugly into the bottom and sides of the pan. Crumble the ladyfingers (sponge fingers) over the bottom.

Warm the apricot preserves (jam) gently in a pan and spread it over the ladyfingers, then arrange the apricot halves on top in concentric circles. Bake for 20–25 minutes. Remove and transfer to a serving plate after a few minutes.

Tip: The ladyfingers can be replaced with 4–5 crumbled rusks or, for a different flavor, with 4 slices of spiced bread (pain d'épices) *reduced to crumbs in a food processor.*

TORTINE CIOCCO-COCCO

CHOCOLATE AND COCONUT TARTLETS

AVERAGE

– Preparation time: *40 minutes*
– Cooking time: *20 minutes*
– Calories per serving: *312*
– *Makes 12*

INGREDIENTS

– flour, for dusting
– 1¼ sticks (5 oz/150 g) butter,
  plus extra for greasing
– ⅔ quantity Basic Pie Dough
  (Shortcrust Pastry), see
  page 105
– 2 cups (5 oz/150 g)
  dry unsweetened
  (dessicated) coconut
– 4 eggs, lightly beaten
– ¾ cup (5 oz/150 g) sugar
– 3½ oz/100 g semisweet
  (dark) chocolate, chopped
– 4 tablespoons heavy
  (double) cream

Preheat the oven to 350°F/180°C/Gas Mark 4 and grease and dust a 12-cup muffin pan. Roll out the basic pie dough (shortcrust pastry) on a lightly floured surface, divide into 12 disks and use them to line the muffin pan.

In a saucepan, melt the butter over low heat, add the dry (desiccated) coconut, eggs, and sugar, and stir well. Transfer the filling to the pan and bake for 20 minutes.

Meanwhile, put the chocolate and cream into a double boiler or a heatproof bowl set over a saucepan of barely simmering water and melt until smooth and fairly thick. Take the tartlets out of the oven, pour the hot chocolate cream over their surfaces, and let set completely. They can be kept in the refrigerator until needed and served at room temperature.

Tip: Freshly grated coconut can also be used for this recipe. To open a coconut, pierce 2 small holes where there are 3 dark marks on the shell, drain the coconut water, and bake the coconut at 350°F/180°C/Gas Mark 4 for 20 minutes. Let cool. When cold, break open. The coconut flesh should detach easily and be ready for grating.

CROSTATA DI LIME AI PINOLI

LIME AND PINE NUT TART

- Preparation time: *20 minutes + 1–2 hours chilling*
- Cooking time: *30 minutes*
- Calories per serving: *584*
- *Serves 4*

INGREDIENTS

- 4 tablespoons (2½ oz/60 g) butter, melted, plus extra for greasing
- 5 oz/150 g graham crackers or digestive biscuits
- 3 egg yolks
- 1¼ cups (11 fl oz/300 ml) evaporated milk
- 2 limes
- ½ cup (2½ oz/60 g) pine nuts
- 1 cup (8 fl oz/250 ml) heavy (double) cream, whipped

Preheat the oven to 350°F/180°C/Gas Mark 4 and grease an 8-inch/20-cm baking pan. Process the cookies (biscuits) to crumbs in a food processor. Pour the melted butter gradually into the cookie crumbs while processing. Spread the mixture in the bottom of the baking pan, pressing down well and making sure it is even, then chill it in the refrigerator for 1–2 hours, until firm.

Blend the egg yolks in a food processor with the evaporated milk, a little grated zest from 1 lime and the juice of both limes. Stir in the pine nuts and pour the mixture into the baking pan.

Bake for 20 minutes. Remove the tart from the oven, let cool, and chill in the refrigerator until you are ready to serve. Just before serving, pour the cream into a bowl and whip until stiff peaks form. Spread the whipped cream on top and grate a little zest over it.

CROSTATA DI FRAGOLE
ALLO ZABAGLIONE
STRAWBERRY AND ZABAGLIONE TART

EASY

– Preparation time: *1 hour*
– Cooking time: *55 minutes*
– Calories per serving: *371*
– *Serves 6*

FOR THE TART

– flour, for dusting
– butter, for greasing
– ½ quantity Basic Pie Dough (Shortcrust Pastry), see page 105
– 3⅓ cups (14 oz/400 g) strawberries, hulled and quartered
– ⅔ cup (5 fl oz/150 ml) Marsala
– ⅓ cup (2½ oz/60 g) sugar
– 8 ladyfingers (sponge fingers)
– 2 egg yolks
– confectioners' (icing) sugar, for dusting

Preheat the oven to 350°F/180°C/Gas Mark 4 and grease and dust a 10-inch/25-cm fluted tart pan. Roll out the basic pie dough (shortcrust pastry) into a disk on a lightly floured surface and line the bottom and sides of the pan with it. Prick the bottom with a fork, cover with parchment (baking) paper and sprinkle with pie weights (baking beans). Bake for 10 minutes.

Meanwhile, mix the strawberries with the Marsala and 1 tablespoon of the sugar in a bowl and let stand. Remove the pastry shell (case) from the oven, discard the parchment paper and weights, and return to the oven for 10 minutes. Take out and let cool. Chop the ladyfingers (sponge fingers) finely and sprinkle them evenly over the bottom of the tart.

Place the strawberries on the layer of crumbs, reserving the Marsala.

To make the zabaglione, whisk the egg yolks with the remaining sugar in a double boiler (or a heatproof bowl over a saucepan of simmering water) over low heat until pale and frothy; do not allow it to boil, or it will curdle. Gradually add the Marsala and continue whisking until the mixture has thickened and coats the back of a spoon. Remove from the heat and let cool.

Preheat the broiler (grill). Spoon the zabaglione over the strawberries, sprinkle with confectioners' (icing) sugar, and broil (grill) the tart, without burning it, for up to 10 minutes, until lightly browned on top. Serve warm.

TARTELETTE ALLE PRUGNE E FORMAGGIO

PLUM AND CHEESE TARTLETS

EASY

– Preparation time: *20 minutes*
– Cooking time: *30 minutes*
– Calories per serving: *457*
– *Serves 4*

INGREDIENTS

– butter, for greasing
– flour, for dusting
– ⅓ quantity Basic Pie Dough (Shortcrust Pastry), see page 105
– 3 eggs
– 1 tablespoon double (heavy) cream
– generous ⅓ cup (3 oz/90 g) cream cheese
– ½ cup (3 oz/90 g) sugar
– few drops of vanilla extract
– 3 small plums, pitted (stoned) and cut into pieces

Preheat the oven to 350°F/180°C/Gas Mark 4 and grease and dust 4 individual tartlet molds. Divide the basic pie dough (shortcrust pastry) into 4 equal pieces. Roll them out, not too thinly, on a lightly floured surface and use them to line the tartlet molds. Cover each one with a square of parchment (baking) paper that has been soaked, squeezed out, and patted dry, and fill with pie weights (baking beans). Bake for 8–10 minutes.

Meanwhile, put the eggs, cream, cream cheese, sugar, and vanilla in a food processor. Process until smooth, add the plum pieces, and process again. When the mixture is evenly blended, divide it among the tartlets and return to the oven for another 20 minutes. Let cool a little before serving warm.

CROSTATA AL FORMAGGIO

CREAM CHEESE TART

AVERAGE

– Preparation time: *30 minutes*
  + 30 minutes chilling
– Cooking time: *45–50 minutes*
– Calories per serving: *480*
– *Serves 6*

INGREDIENTS

– ½ stick (2 oz/50 g) softened
  butter, plus extra for greasing
– 9 oz/250 g Basic Pie Dough
  (Shortcrust Pastry), see
  page 105
– flour, for dusting
– 2 tablespoons raisins
– 1½ cups (12 oz/350 g)
  cream cheese
– generous ½ cup (4 oz/100 g)
  sugar
– 2 eggs
– 2 tablespoons light (single)
  cream
– 1 teaspoon ground cinnamon
– 1 teaspoon grated lemon zest
– confectioners' (icing) sugar,
  for dusting

Preheat the oven to 350°F/180°C/Gas Mark 4 and grease a 4 x 10-inch/10 x 25-cm rectangular baking pan. Roll out the basic pie dough (shortcrust pastry) on a lightly floured surface to a thickness of about ¼ inch/6 mm, use it to line the baking pan, and chill it in the refrigerator for 30 minutes. Meanwhile, soak the raisins in warm water.

Prick the bottom of the pastry shell (case) with the prongs of a fork, cover it with a sheet of aluminum foil, and fill it with pie weights (baking beans). Bake for 10 minutes. Remove from the oven, remove the foil and weights, and bake for another 5–10 minutes, until the pastry is golden. Remove and let cool. Reduce the oven temperature to 325°F/160°C/Gas Mark 3.

Meanwhile, drain and gently squeeze the raisins dry. Cream the butter with the cream cheese and sugar, then add the eggs, one at a time, cream, cinnamon, lemon zest, and raisins.

Spread the filling over the pastry, return to the oven, and bake for 30 minutes, or until the filling is firm. Remove and let cool. Dust with confectioners' (icing) sugar and sprinkle with grated lemon zest.

Tip:With a conventional oven, you can avoid blind-baking the pastry by baking it on the lowest rack in the oven, so that the heat is concentrated on the bottom of the baking pan and will cook the pastry, even with a moist filling.

CROSTATA RIPIENA DI CREMA E SPICCHI DI LIMONE
LEMON AND FRANGIPANE TART

AVERAGE

– Preparation time: *30 minutes*
  + 12 hours chilling
– Cooking time: *40 minutes*
– Calories per serving: 766
– *Serves 8*

FOR THE PASTRY

– 3 eggs
– 2 teaspoons sugar
– 1¼ sticks (5 oz/150 g) butter,
  softened
– 2⅓ cups (11 oz/300 g)
  all-purpose (plain) flour,
  plus extra for dusting
– few drops of vanilla extract
– grated zest of 1 lemon

FOR THE CUSTARD

– 1 stick (4 oz/125 g) butter
– 1¼ cups (4 oz/125 g) ground
  almonds (almond meal)
– 2 eggs
– 1 cup (4 oz/125 g)
  confectioners' (icing) sugar

FOR THE PASTRY CREAM

– 2 cups (16 fl oz/475 ml) milk
– 2 unwaxed lemons
– 1 vanilla bean
– 4 egg yolks
– ½ cup (3½ oz/100 g) sugar
– 3 tablespoons all-purpose
  (plain) flour
– 3 tablespoons cornstarch
  (cornflour)

To make the dough, whisk 2 eggs with the sugar and butter, then add the flour, vanilla extract, and lemon zest and bring together to form a soft dough. Wrap the pastry in plastic wrap (clingfilm) and chill it overnight in the refrigerator.

Preheat the oven to 400°F/200°C/Gas Mark 6 and grease and dust an 11-inch/28-cm round baking pan. Make the almond custard: Blend the butter and almonds in a food processor at the maximum speed, then add the eggs, one at a time. Mix in the confectioners' (icing) sugar. Set aside.

Make the pastry cream. Bring the milk slowly to a boil in a heavy saucepan with a strip of lemon zest and the vanilla bean, stir, and set aside. In a large heatproof bowl placed over a saucepan of simmering water, whisk the egg yolks with the sugar until pale and frothy. Stir continuously as you gradually sift in the flour and cornstarch (cornflour). Strain the milk and reheat it, then add it in a thin stream to the egg yolk mixture, stirring continuously, and cook for 5 minutes. Remove from the heat and let cool.

Roll out three-quarters of the pastry into a disk on a lightly floured surface, place the disk inside the pan, cover with foil and sprinkle with pie weights (baking beans). Bake for 10 minutes, then reduce the oven temperature to 325°F/160°C/Gas Mark 3. Remove the shell (case) from the oven and remove the weights and foil.

Cut out segments from the lemons and grate the zest. Mix the almond custard with the pastry cream, grated lemon zest and segments and fill the pastry shell with the mixture. Brush the lid with the remaining egg, beaten, and bake for 25 minutes. Serve the tart warm, dusted with confectioners' sugar.

CROSTATA AL CIOCCOLATO
E LAMPONI
CHOCOLATE AND RASPBERRY TART

EASY

– Preparation time: *15 minutes*
– Cooking time: *30 minutes*
– Calories per serving: *735*
– *Serves 6*

INGREDIENTS

– 4½ oz/125 g semisweet
  (dark) chocolate
– 2 eggs, lightly beaten
– ⅓ cup (2½ fl oz/75 ml)
  light (single) cream
– ½ quantity Basic Pie Dough
  (Shortcrust Pastry), see
  page 105
– flour, for dusting
– ¾ cup (4½ oz/125 g)
  raspberries
– ¾ cup (3 oz/80 g)
  confectioners' (icing) sugar

Preheat the oven to 400°F/200°C/Gas Mark 6 and line a 10-inch/25-cm rectangular baking pan with parchment (baking) paper. Break up the chocolate and melt it gently in a double boiler or a heatproof bowl set over a saucepan of barely simmering water, stirring occasionally, then remove from the heat. Add the eggs and cream and stir carefully.

Meanwhile, roll out the basic pie dough (shortcrust pastry) on a lightly floured surface and use it to line the bottom and sides of the baking pan and prick the bottom with a fork. Chill in the refrigerator for 30 minutes.

Pour the chocolate filling onto the pastry shell (case) and bake for 25 minutes. Remove, let cool, and lay the raspberries on top. Dust with confectioners' (icing) sugar, transfer to a serving plate, and serve.

CROSTATA DI PERE E CREMA DI MANDORLE

PEAR AND FRANGIPANE TART

- Preparation time: *15 minutes*
- Cooking time: *40 minutes*
- Calories per serving: *747*
- *Serves 6*

FOR THE TART

- 4 Bartlett (Williams) pears
- juice of 1 lemon
- ⅔ quantity Basic Pie Dough (Shortcrust Pastry), see page 105
- flour, for dusting
- ⅓ cup (1¼ oz/30 g) slivered (flaked) almonds
- ⅓ cup (3½ oz/100 g) apricot preserves (jam)

FOR THE CUSTARD

- 6 tablespoons (3 oz/80 g) butter
- ¾ cup (3 oz/80 g) ground almonds (almond meal)
- 6 tablespoons sugar
- 2 eggs
- 4 teaspoons pear liqueur

FOR THE SYRUP

- 1 cup (7 oz/200 g) sugar

Preheat the oven to 400°F/200°C/Gas Mark 6 and line a 10-inch/25-cm baking pan with parchment (baking) paper.

Make the syrup. Pour 1¼ cups (11 fl oz/300 ml) water into a heavy saucepan, add the sugar, and cook over medium heat, stirring, until the mixture has a syrupy pouring consistency.

Meanwhile, peel the pears, cut them into quarters, remove the cores, and sprinkle with a little lemon juice. Plunge them into the boiling syrup, add the remaining lemon juice, and cook for 5 minutes.

Make the custard. Melt the butter over medium-low heat or in a double boiler, then set aside to cool slightly. Mix the ground almonds (almond meal) in a bowl with the sugar and eggs. Stir in the lukewarm melted butter and the pear liqueur. Drain the pears and thinly slice them lengthwise.

On a lightly floured surface, roll out the basic pie dough (shortcrust pastry) into a disk and line the bottom and sides of the baking pan with it. Pour in the custard, arrange the pear slices in circles on top, and sprinkle with the slivered (flaked) almonds. Bake for 25 minutes.

Heat the apricot preserves (jam) in a small saucepan and pour over the warm tart as a glaze. Serve warm or cold.

CROSTATA DI NOCI ALLO SCIROPPO D'ACERO

MAPLE PECAN TART

EASY

– Preparation time: *20 minutes*
– Cooking time: *1 hour 5 minutes*
– Calories per serving: *570*
– *Serves 6*

INGREDIENTS

– butter, for greasing
– ½ Basic Pie Dough
  (Shortcrust Pastry), see
  page 105
– flour, for dusting
– 1½ cups (6 oz/175 g)
  pecans
– 2 eggs
– 2 tablespoons (1¼ oz/30 g)
  butter
– ½ cup (4 fl oz/120 ml) light
  (single) cream
– ½ cup (4 oz/120 g) brown
  sugar
– ½ cup (4 fl oz/120 ml)
  maple syrup
– ⅓ cup (2½ fl oz/75 ml) rum
– 1 teaspoon vanilla extract
– salt

Preheat the oven to 350°F/180°C/Gas Mark 4 and grease a 10-inch/25-cm fluted tart pan. Roll out the basic pie dough (shortcrust pastry) into a disk on a lightly floured surface and use it to line the bottom and sides of the baking pan. Cover the bottom with aluminum foil, fill with pie weights (baking beans) and bake for 10 minutes. Remove, discard the foil and baking beans, and return to the oven for 5–10 minutes.

Chop half the pecans and leave the rest whole. Blend the eggs, the chopped nuts, butter, cream, sugar, maple syrup, rum, vanilla extract, and a pinch of salt in a food processor at medium speed—do not overblend or the butter may split.

Pour the blended mixture into the pastry shell (case), decorate with the remaining nuts, and bake for 45 minutes.

CROSTATA DI PERE
AL VINO ROSSO
PEAR AND RED WINE TART

EASY

– Preparation time: *20 minutes*
– Cooking time: *55 minutes–*
  1 hour
– Calories per serving: *455*
– *Serves 6*

INGREDIENTS

– butter, for greasing
– flour, for dusting
– ½ quantity Basic Pie Dough
  (Shortcrust Pastry), see
  page 105
– 4 pears
– 1⅔ cups (14 fl oz/400 ml)
  red wine
– grated zest of ½ unwaxed
  lemon
– 4½ tablespoons sugar
– 4 cloves

Preheat the oven to 350°F/180°C/Gas Mark 4 and grease and dust a 9-inch/23-cm fluted tart pan. Roll out the basic pie dough (shortcrust pastry) into a disk on a lightly floured surface and use it to line the bottom and sides of the baking pan. Cover the bottom with aluminum foil, fill with pie weights (baking beans), and bake for 15 minutes. Remove and discard the foil and weights and return to the oven for another 5–10 minutes, then remove and let cool.

Meanwhile, peel the pears and arrange in a heavy saucepan, then add the wine, the lemon zest, sugar, cloves, and a scant 1 cup (7 fl oz/200 ml) water. Cover and cook gently for 30 minutes. When the pears are cooked, carefully lift them out and let cool.

Boil the cooking liquid and reduce it to a syrup, then remove and strain it. Thinly slice the pears and, starting from the outermost edge of the tart, arrange them so that they fan out from the center in a circle in the pastry shell (case). Drizzle with 2–3 tablespoons of the wine syrup and serve.

CROSTATINE MERINGATE
AL LIMONE
LEMON MERINGUE TARTLETS

AVERAGE

– Preparation time: *15 minutes*
– Cooking time: *20 minutes*
– Calories per serving: *390*
– *Makes 12*

INGREDIENTS

– 4 unwaxed lemons
– 3 eggs plus 2 egg yolks
– 1 cup (7 oz/200 g) sugar, plus 1 tablespoon
– 7 tablespoons (3½ oz/100 g) butter, softened, cut into pieces
– flour, for dusting
– ⅓ quantity Basic Pie Dough (Shortcrust Pastry), or see page 105
– ½ cup (3½ oz/100 g) superfine (caster) sugar

Preheat the oven to 350°F/180°C/Gas Mark 4, cut out 12 squares of parchment (baking) paper, moisten and squeeze them dry, and use them to line twelve 2½-inch/6-cm tartlet pans.

Squeeze the juice from 3 of the lemons and measure out ½ cup (4 fl oz/120 ml) juice. Separate 2 eggs and reserve the whites. Put 4 egg yolks, a whole egg, the sugar, and butter in a Dutch oven (casserole dish) or heavy saucepan and cook over low heat 10 minutes, stirring constantly, until it comes to a boil and has thickened. Pour the lemon curd into a bowl and cool it quickly by partly submerging the bowl in cold water.

Roll out the basic pie dough (shortcrust pastry) on a lightly floured surface to about ⅛ in/3 mm thick. Line the prepared tartlet pans with the dough, fill with pie weights (baking beans) and bake for about 10 minutes. Remove the parchment paper and weight and bake for another 2–3 minutes or until golden.

Let the pastry shells (cases) cool, then fill them with the lemon curd and chill in the refrigerator. Preheat the oven to its highest setting. Whisk the 2 reserved egg whites with the 1 tablespoon caster (superfine) sugar until you have a glossy and firm meringue with stiff peaks. Spoon or pipe it on top of the lemon curd, covering it completely. Bake for 2–3 minutes, until the meringue has browned. Let cool before serving.

Tip: The pastry shells and the lemon curd can be made 24–48 hours in advance, but it is best to assemble the tartlets and prepare the meringue just before serving.

CROSTATA CON GANACHE AL CIOCCOLATO
CHOCOLATE GANACHE TART

INGREDIENTS

– 7 oz/200 g semisweet (dark) chocolate, finely chopped
– 1 cup (8 fl oz/250 ml) heavy (double) cream
– 1½ tablespoons (¾ oz/20 g) butter, cut into small pieces
– ½ quantity Basic Pie Dough (Shortcrust Pastry), see page 105
– unsweetened cocoa powder, for dusting

Preheat the oven to 350°F/180°C/Gas Mark 4. Put the chocolate into a double boiler or heatproof bowl set over a saucepan of barely simmering water, along with the cream, and let it melt gently. Stir well and add the butter, then stir until it has melted.

Roll out the basic pie dough (shortcrust pastry) between 2 sheets of parchment (baking) paper to a thickness of ⅛ inch/3 mm.

Discard the parchment paper and line an 8-inch/20-cm baking pan with the pastry. Cut off any excess, prick the bottom with a fork, and cover with moistened parchment paper that has been squeezed dry. Fill it with baking beans (pie weights) and bake for about 15 minutes. Remove the parchment paper and weight and cook for another 5–6 minutes.

Let the pastry shell (case) cool, then pour the prepared ganache into it and chill the tart in the refrigerator for at least 2 hours. Dust liberally with sifted cocoa powder and serve.

Tip: For variations on this recipe, flavor the ganache with 1 heaping teaspoon ground cinnamon to the chocolate and cream mixture before melting them; or 1 teaspoon of instant coffee; grated orange zest; or a pinch of chili powder.

FILLED PASTRIES

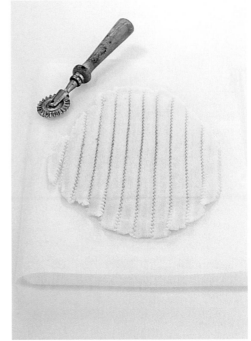

TECHNIQUE

CROSTATA A INCROCIO CON MARMELLATA

JAM PIE

EASY

– Preparation time: *20 minutes*
  + 30 minutes chilling
– Cooking time: *30 minutes*
– Calories per serving: *560*
– *Serves 6*

INGREDIENTS

– butter, for greasing
– 1 quantity Basic Pie Dough
  (Shortcrust Pastry), see
  page 105
– all-purple (plain) flour,
  for dusting
– juice of ½ lemon, strained
– 1¼ cups (12 oz/350 g)
  strawberry preserves (jam)
– milk, for brushing
– confectioners' (icing) sugar,
  for dusting

STEP 1

Preheat the oven to 350°F/180°C/Gas Mark 4 and grease an 8-inch/20-cm fluted tart pan with a removable bottom. Set aside one-third of the basic pie dough (shortcrust pastry) and roll out the remainder to about ¼ inch/5 mm thick on a lightly floured surface, then transfer to the baking pan. Press down well on the bottom and sides and cut off any excess dough with a small sharp knife. Prick the bottom with a fork and put the pan in the refrigerator and chill for 30 minutes.

STEP 2

Roll out the reserved dough and the scraps (offcuts) on a sheet of parchment (baking) paper to ⅛ inch/3 mm. Cut into strips about ⅜ inch/1 cm wide with a ridged pastry wheel. Put the parchment paper and pastry strips in the freezer for 5 minutes.

STEP 3

Mix the lemon juice with the preserves and fill the shell (case) with the mixture. Take the pastry strips out of the freezer and arrange them on top of the preserves in a lattice pattern.

STEP 4

Trim the pastry strips, then stick the strips onto the pastry edges around the sides, pressing down with a finger, and brush the dough with milk. Bake for about 30 minutes. Let cool a little, then transfer to a cooling rack to cool completely before serving. Dust with just a little confectioners' (icing) sugar.

TORTA RIPIENA ALLE MELE

APPLE STRUDEL

AVERAGE

- Preparation time: *20 minutes*
  + 30 minutes resting
- Cooking time: *45 minutes*
- Calories per serving: *486*
- *Serves 8*

FOR THE PASTRY

- 2¼ cups (9 oz/250 g)
  all-purpose (plain) flour,
  plus extra for dusting
- 7 tablespoons (3½ oz/100 g)
  butter, melted, plus extra for
  greasing
- 1 egg
- ½ cup (3½ oz/100 g) sugar
- salt

FOR THE FILLING

- ¼ cup (1¼ oz/35 g) raisins
- 2½ tablespoons (1¼ oz/35 g)
  butter, softened
- 2 eggs, separated
- ¼ cup (2 oz/50 g) sugar
- scant ½ cup (3½ fl oz/
  100 ml) heavy (double)
  cream
- ⅓ cup (1 oz/30 g) dried
  bread crumbs
- pinch of ground cinnamon
- ⅓ cup (2 oz/50 g) grapes,
  chopped
- 2–3 apples, very thinly sliced
- 1 tablespoon pine nuts
- 2½ tablespoons (1¼ oz/
  30 g) melted butter
- milk, for brushing
- confectioners' (icing) sugar

Sift the flour into a mound on a clean work surface, make a well in the center, and add the butter, egg, sugar, a pinch of salt, and 6 tablespoons water. Gradually incorporate them into the flour and bring together to form a smooth elastic dough. Cover and chill for 30 minutes. Meanwhile, soak the raisins in a bowl of lukewarm water.

Preheat the oven to 425°F/220°C/Gas Mark 7 and grease a baking sheet. Drain the raisins and dry them on paper towels. Cream the softened butter with the egg yolks and sugar in a bowl. Add the cream, bread crumbs, raisins, ground cinnamon, and grapes. In a separate bowl, whisk the egg whites to stiff peaks and fold them in.

Roll out the pastry dough thinly into a large rectangle on a lightly floured surface and transfer to a large piece of plastic wrap (clingfilm) dusted with flour (this will make it easier to roll up the dough into a cylinder). Arrange the filling on the dough and sprinkle the apples and pine nuts on top. Roll up the dough into a fat cylindrical shape, brush the top with the melted butter, and place on the baking sheet. Bake for about 45 minutes. Halfway through the cooking time, brush the strudel with milk and reduce the oven temperature to 350°F/180°C/Gas Mark 4. Remove from the oven, transfer a serving dish, and dust liberally with confectioners' (icing) sugar.

CROSTATA DI RICOTTA

RICOTTA TART

– Preparation time: *35 minutes
  + 30 minutes chilling*
– Cooking time: *35–40 minutes*
– Calories per serving: *631*
– *Serves 8–10*

FOR THE PASTRY

– 1¼ sticks (5 oz/150 g) soft
  butter, softened and cut into
  small pieces, plus extra for
  greasing
– 2⅓ cups (11 oz/300 g)
  all-purpose (plain) flour
– ¾ cup (5 oz/150 g) sugar
– grated zest of 1 unwaxed
  lemon
– 1 egg plus 2 egg yolks

FOR THE FILLING

– 1¾ cups (14 oz/400 g)
  ricotta cheese
– 4 eggs
– ½ tablespoon all-purpose
  (plain) flour
– ⅓ cup plus 1 tablespoon
  (3 oz/80 g) sugar
– 2 tablespoons raisins
– 2 tablespoons pine nuts
– 2 tablespoons candied
  (glacé) peel
– pinch of ground cinnamon
– grated zest of 1 unwaxed
  orange and 1 unwaxed
  lemon
– confectioners' (icing) sugar,
  for dusting
– salt

Preheat the oven to 375°F/190°C/Gas Mark 5, grease a 10-inch/25-cm baking pan with butter.

Make the pastry dough. Sift the flour into a mound on a clean work surface, make a well in it, and add the sugar, and lemon zest. Crack the whole egg into the center and add the egg yolks and butter. Using your hands, mix these gradually into the dry ingredients until a dough comes together, then cover with plastic wrap (clingfilm) and chill the dough in the refrigerator for 30 minutes.

Meanwhile, make the filling. Push the ricotta cheese through a strainer (sieve) into a bowl, separate 3 eggs (reserve the whites) and mix the ricotta with the 3 egg yolks, whole egg, and remaining ingredients.

In a separate bowl, whisk the 3 egg whites to stiff peaks and fold them into the mixture. Roll out the dough into 2 disks, one slightly smaller than the other.

Place the larger pastry disk inside the prepared baking pan, making it come up the sides, and spread the ricotta filling on top. Cut the other disk into strips with a fluted pastry wheel. Lay these in a lattice pattern over the ricotta filling. Beat the remaining egg and use it to brush over the dough. Bake for 35–40 minutes. Remove from the oven and transfer to a serving plate. Dust with confectioners' (icing) sugar.

CROSTATA DI CILIEGIE

CHERRY PIE

AVERAGE

– Preparation time: *20 minutes*
– Cooking time: *30* minutes
– Calories per serving: *594*
– *Serves 6*

INGREDIENTS

– butter, for dusting
– flour, for dusting
– 1 quantity Basic Pie Dough
  (Shortcrust Pastry), see
  page 105
– 1¼ cups (12 oz/350 g)
  cherry preserves (jam)
– juice of ½ lemon
– 1 egg yolk, lightly beaten

Preheat the oven to 350°F/180°C/Gas Mark 4 and butter and dust a 10-inch/25-cm fluted tart pan. Cut off one- third of the basic pie dough (shortcrust pastry) for the lattice strips and roll out the remainder into a thin disk on a lightly floured surface. Use the dough to line the bottom and sides of the pan.

Combine the preserves (jam) and lemon juice, then transfer it into the pastry shell (case) with the jam. Roll out the reserved dough, cut it into strips, and place these over the top in a lattice. Brush it with egg yolk. Bake for 30 minutes. Remove from the oven, let cool, then serve at room temperature.

TORTA ARROTOLATA ALL'ALSAZIANA
ALSACE-STYLE STRUDEL

– Preparation time: *45 minutes*
– Cooking time: *45–50 minutes*
– Calories per serving: *523*
– *Serves 8*

INGREDIENTS

– 4 tablespoons (2 oz/60 g)
  butter, melted, plus extra
  for greasing
– 1¾ lb/750 g apples
– ½ cup (4 oz/100 g) sugar
– 1¾ cups (14 oz/400 g)
  ricotta
– 2 eggs plus 1 egg, separated
– 1 lb/500 g ready-to-bake
  puff pastry
– ⅓ cup (2 oz/50 g)
  poppy seeds
– milk, for brushing
– confectioners' (icing) sugar,
  for dusting

Preheat the oven to 325°F/160°C/Gas Mark 3 and grease a deep rectangular baking pan measuring about 10 x 13 inches/25 x 35-cm. Peel and chop the apples and put them into a heavy saucepan with half the sugar and a scant ½ cup (3½ fl oz/100 ml) water and cook gently over medium-low heat. In a bowl, combine the ricotta, whole eggs, the extra egg yolk, and remaining sugar. Beat the egg white to stiff peaks. Beat well, and when the mixture is frothy, fold in the egg white.

Roll 2 sheets of puff pastry thicker and bigger than the baking pan and the other 2 sheets thinner and to the size of the pan. Line the baking pan with one of the thicker sheets and brush with melted butter.

Pour the ricotta mixture into the pastry-lined baking pan. Cover it with a thin sheet of pastry, brush with melted butter, then sprinkle about half the poppy seeds on top. Cover with another thin sheet of pastry, brush with melted butter, and arrange the cooked apples on top. Cover with the remaining thick sheet of pastry and carefully pinch the edges together to seal. Brush with a little milk.

Bake for 45–50 minutes. Remove from the oven and transfer to a serving plate. Dust with confectioners' (icing) sugar and sprinkle with the remaining poppy seeds. Serve warm.

TORTA RIPIENA CON RICOTTA E AMARENE

RICOTTA AND CHERRY STRUDEL

AVERAGE

– Preparation time: *30 minutes
+ 1 hour resting*
– Cooking time: *45 minutes*
– Calories per serving: *521–391*
– *Serves 6–8*

FOR THE PASTRY

– 2 cups (9 oz/250 g)
all-purpose (plain) flour,
plus extra for dusting
– 1 egg
– 2 tablespoons oil
– salt

FOR THE FILLING

– 2¼ cups (1 lb 2 oz/500 g)
ricotta
– ½ cup (3½ oz/100 g) sugar
– 3 eggs
– pinch of ground cinnamon
– 1 tablespoon grated lemon
zest
– 2½ tablespoons (1¼ oz/30 g)
butter, melted
– bread crumbs, for sprinkling
– 3–4 tablespoons cherries
in syrup
– confectioners' (icing) sugar,
for dusting

Make the pastry: sift the flour into a mound on a clean work surface, make a well in the center, and add the eggs, oil, and a pinch of salt. Gradually incorporate them into the flour, adding a little lukewarm water, if necessary, and bring together to form a smooth elastic dough. Fill a large bowl with boiling water, let stand for a minute, then empty it and dry it and immediately invert it over the dough. Let rest for about 1 hour.

Preheat the oven to 350°F/180°C/Gas Mark 4 and line a large baking pan with moistened parchment (baking) paper. Make the filling. Push the ricotta through a strainer (sieve) and transfer it to a bowl, add the sugar, eggs, one at a time, ground cinnamon, and lemon zest and mix until smooth and even. Roll out the dough to a thickness of ½ inch/1 cm on a lightly floured surface and place it on a large, clean dish towel.

Using your fingertips, very gently stretch out the dough around the edges without tearing it, to make a border of thinner dough. Leaving the thinned borders uncovered, brush the dough with some of the butter and sprinkle with bread crumbs. Drain the cherries. Spread the ricotta filling on a quarter of the dough and arrange the cherries on top. Using the dish towel, roll up the dough like a jelly (Swiss) roll.

Place the strudel in the baking pan, bending it to form a wide horseshoe shape. Brush it with butter and bake for 40 minutes. Remove, let cool, transfer to a serving dish, and dust with confectioners' (icing) sugar.

CROSTATA DI MANDORLE

ALMOND LATTICE PIE

– Preparation time: *20 minutes*
  + 2–3 hours chilling time
– Cooking time: *30 minutes*
– Calories per serving: *706*
– *Serves 8*

FOR THE PASTRY

– 2⅓ cups (11 oz/300 g)
  all-purpose (plain) flour,
  sifted, plus extra for dusting
– ¾ cup (5 oz/150 g) sugar
– 1¼ sticks (5 oz/150 g) butter,
  cut into cubes, plus extra for
  greasing
– 2 eggs
– zest of 1 lemon
– vanilla extract
– salt

FOR THE FILLING

– 2 egg whites
– 3 (¾ lb/300 g) chopped
  almonds
– 1 cup (7 oz/200 g) sugar
– grated zest of 1 unwaxed
  lemon

Put the flour into a food processor with the sugar, butter, and a pinch of salt and process in a food processor until the mixture resembles bread crumbs. Add the eggs, lemon zest, and vanilla and pulse until a dough ball is formed. Wrap in plastic wrap (clingfilm) and let it chill in the refrigerator for 2–3 hours.

Preheat the oven to 350°F/180°C/Gas Mark 4 and grease and dust an 8-inch/20-cm round baking pan. Roll out the dough into a disk on a lightly floured surface and use it to line the pan. Reserve any scraps to make the lattice. Cover the bottom with a sheet of parchment (baking) paper that has been rinsed and squeezed dry, fill with some pie weights (baking beans), and bake for about 10 minutes. Reduce the oven temperature to 325°F/160°C/Gas Mark 3.

Meanwhile, whisk the egg whites to stiff peaks and fold in the almonds, sugar, and lemon zest. Spoon this filling into the pastry shell (case). Cut the reserved dough into strips and lay them on top in a lattice pattern, then bake for 20 minutes. Remove, let cool, and serve.

TORTA ARROTOLATA DI NOCI

WALNUT STRUDEL

- Preparation time: *30 minutes*
  + 1 hour resting
- Cooking time: *30 minutes*
- Calories per serving: *503*
- *Serves 6*

FOR THE PASTRY

- 2 cups (9 oz/250 g)
  all-purpose (plain) flour,
  plus extra for dusting
- 1 egg
- 2 tablespoons oil
- 1 egg yolk beaten with a little
  milk, to glaze
- salt

FOR THE FILLING

- 1²⁄₃ cups (7 oz/200 g)
  walnuts, skinned (see tip)
  and finely chopped
- scant 1 cup (7 fl oz/200 ml)
  milk
- ²⁄₃ cup (5 oz/150 g) honey
- grated zest of 1 unwaxed
  lemon

Make the pastry dough. Sift the flour into a mound on a clean work surface, make a well in the center, and add the egg, oil, and a pinch of salt. Gradually incorporate them into the flour, adding a little lukewarm water, if necessary, and bring together to form a smooth dough. Pour boiling water into a large bowl to heat it, then dry it and place upside down over the dough, making sure it covers it well, and let it rest for about 1 hour.

Preheat the oven to 350°F/180°C/Gas Mark 4 and line a baking pan with moistened parchment (baking) paper. Mix the walnuts with the milk, honey, and lemon zest in a bowl.

Roll out the dough to a thickness of ½ inch/1 cm, using very little flour, then place the dough on a large clean dish towel and, using your fingertips, gently stretch it out around the edges without tearing it, to make a border of thinner dough. Spread out the walnut filling without covering the thin borders. Use the dish towel to help you roll up the dough around the filling, as if making a jelly (Swiss) roll.

Place the strudel in the baking pan, bending it to form a wide horseshoe shape. Brush it with the egg yolk and milk mixture and bake for about 30 minutes. Remove and let it for 5 minutes. Serve in slices, warm or at room temperature.

Tip: To skin the walnuts, scald them for 1 minute in boiling water, then drain and skin them while still warm.

CROSTATA DI ZUCCA

PUMPKIN PIE

EASY

– Preparation time: *40 minutes*
– Cooking time: *55 minutes–
  1 hour 5 minutes*
– Calories per serving: *369*
– *Serves 6*

INGREDIENTS

– butter, for greasing
– ½ quantity Basic Pie Dough
  (Shortcrust Pastry), or see
  page 105)
– all-purpose (plain) flour,
  for dusting
– 2 eggs
– ⅔ cup (5 oz/150 g) packed
  brown sugar
– 2¼ cups (1 lb 2 oz/500 g)
  pumpkin puree
– ½ cup (4 fl oz/120 ml)
  double (heavy) cream
– 1 tablespoon sherry
– pinch of ground cinnamon
– pinch of ground nutmeg
– pinch of ground ginger
– salt
– vanilla ice cream, to serve

Preheat the oven to 350°F/180°C/Gas Mark 4 and grease an 8-inch/20-cm round baking pan.

Roll out the basic pie dough (shortcrust pastry) into a disk on a lightly floured surface, reserving a small portion for decoration, and line the bottom and sides of the baking pan with it. Cover the bottom with aluminum foil, fill with pie weights (baking beans), and bake for 10 minutes. Remove, discard the foil and weights, and return to the oven for another 5–10 minutes.

Roll out the reserved dough and cut out leaf-shaped decorations. Beat the eggs and the sugar in a bowl until pale and frothy. Add the pumpkin puree, cream, sherry, ground spices, and a pinch of salt.

Pour the mixture into the pastry shell (case), arrange the pastry leaves on top, cover with pricked aluminum foil, and bake for 20 minutes. Discard the foil and cook for another 20–25 minutes. Serve the pie warm or at room temperature, with vanilla ice cream on the side.

TORTA ARROTOLATA DI UVETTA, ALBICOCCHE E FICHE SECCHI

RAISIN, APRICOT, AND FIG STRUDEL

INGREDIENTS

– 11 oz/320 g ready-to-bake puff pastry
– flour, for dusting
– ⅔ cup (3½ oz/100 g) raisins
– 6 dried apricots
– 4 dried figs
– ⅔ cup (1½ oz/40 g) fresh bread crumbs
– 2 tablespoons (1¼ oz/30 g) honey
– 2 tablespoons (1 oz/25 g) butter, softened
– 1 egg, beaten, plus 1 egg yolk
– ¼ cup (2 oz/50 g) sugar
– ¼ cup (2 fl oz/50 ml) heavy (double) cream
– grated zest of 1 unwaxed lemon
– confectioners' (icing) sugar, for dusting

Preheat the oven to 400°F/200°C/Gas Mark 6 and line a baking sheet with parchment (baking) paper. Soak the raisins in lukewarm water for at least 20 minutes, then drain, squeeze, and pat dry on paper towels.

Make the filling. Coarsely chop the apricots and figs and mix them with the bread crumbs, raisins, and honey. In a separate bowl, stir the softened butter into the egg yolks, sugar, cream, lemon zest and add the dried fruit mixture. Mix well.

Roll out the puff pastry on a lightly floured surface to an 8 x 10-inch/20 x 25-cm rectangle, about ⅛ inch/ 3 mm thick, and spread the dried fruit filling on top, over the short edge, leaving the ends uncovered. Roll up the pastry and seal the edges well. Prick the exposed pastry several times with a fork. Place the strudel on the baking sheet and chill, about 30 minutes, until firm. Brush with the egg yolk and bake for 25 minutes. Remove and transfer it to a serving plate after a few minutes. Serve warm, dusted with confectioners' (icing) sugar.

CROSTATA DI PERE E CIOCCOLATO

PEAR AND CHOCOLATE PIE

AVERAGE

– Preparation time: *30 minutes*
  + 1 hour chilling
– Cooking time: *45 minutes*
– Calories per serving: *485*
– *Serves 8*

INGREDIENTS

– 2 sticks (8 oz/225 g) butter,
  plus extra for greasing
– 4½ cups (1 lb/450 g)
  all-purpose (plain) flour,
  plus extra for dusting
– ¼ cup (1 oz/25 g)
  unsweetened cocoa powder
– generous ½ cup (4 oz/120 g)
  sugar
– 1 egg
– 3–4 amaretti cookies
  (biscuits), finely crumbled
  (about ¾ cup)
– 1¾ lb/800 g pears, such as
  Bosc or similar, peeled
  and diced
– confectioners' (icing) sugar,
  for dusting

Grease and dust a shallow 9-inch/23-cm baking pan. Mix the butter, flour, cocoa powder, sugar, and egg in a bowl to make a smooth dough and let rest in a cool place.

Roll out a little more than half the dough into a disk on a lightly floured surface, line the baking pan with it and sprinkle the bottom with finely crumbled dry cookies (biscuits) and the pears.

Roll out the remaining dough into a disk for the lid, place it on the pie and press down well on the edges to seal. Cover the baking pan with plastic wrap (clingfilm) and chill in the refrigerator for 1 hour, or until firm.

Preheat the oven to 375°F/190°C/Gas Mark 5. Remove and discard the wrap and bake for 40–45 minutes.

Remove from the oven and let cool. Transfer to a serving dish and dust the top with confectioners' (icing) sugar.

Tip: The dry cookies in this recipe can be replaced with 5–6 crumbled macaroons, which go very well with pears and chocolate.

CROSTATA DI PISTACCHI
AL CIOCCOLATO AMARO
PISTACHIO AND CHOCOLATE PIE

EASY

– Preparation time: *30 minutes*
– Cooking time: *50 minutes*
– Calories per serving: *636–424*
– *Serves 4–6*

INGREDIENTS

– 3 egg yolks
– 4½ tablespoons sugar
– ¼ cup (1¼ oz/35 g)
  all-purpose (plain) flour
– ⅔ cup (3 oz/80 g) skinned
  and chopped pistachios
– 1⅔ cups (14 fl oz/400 ml)
  milk, plus extra for brushing
– 1 tablespoon rum
– 1½ oz/40 g semisweet (dark)
  chocolate, very finely chopped
– 2 tablespoons (¾ oz/20 g)
  candied orange peel,
  chopped
– butter, for greasing
– flour, for dusting
– ½ quantity Basic Pie Dough
  (Shortcrust Pastry), or see
  page 105)

Beat the egg yolks with the sugar in a heavy saucepan until pale and frothy, then add the flour and pistachios. Heat the milk to boiling point in a separate saucepan and add it to the egg mixture in a thin stream, stirring continuously. Place over low heat and continue stirring until the mixture thickens and coats the back of the spoon. Remove from the heat, add the rum, let cool, then stir in the chocolate and candied orange peel.

Preheat the oven to 350°F/180°C/Gas Mark 4 and grease and dust a 9-inch/23-cm round baking pan. Set aside a small amount of dough for the lattice and roll the main portion into a disk on a lightly floured surface. Use it to line the baking pan and prick the bottom with a fork. Fill it with the cold pistachio and chocolate mixture. Cut the reserved dough into strips and lay them on top in a lattice pattern, brush them with a little milk, and cook in a hot oven, preheated to, for 30 minutes. Take out of the oven, let cool and serve.

CROSTATA DI RICOTTA GARFAGNINA

RICOTTA, RAISIN, AND MARSALA PIE

EASY

– Preparation time:
 *30 minutes + 30 minutes
 soaking*
– Cooking time: *1 hour*
– Calories per serving: *458*
– *Serves 6*

INGREDIENTS

– ½ cup (2½ oz/70 g) raisins
– 4 tablespoons Marsala
– 2¼ cups (1 lb 2 oz/500 g)
 ricotta
– ½ cup (3½ oz/100 g) sugar
– 1 tablespoon all-purpose
 (plain) flour
– 4 eggs, separated
– scant ½ cup (3½ fl oz/
 100 ml) light (single) cream
– grated zest of 1 unwaxed
 lemon
– 1 teaspoon lemon juice
– ½ quantity Basic Pie Dough
 (Shortcrust Pastry), or see
 page 105

Preheat the oven to 350–375°F/180–190°C/Gas Mark 4–5 and line a round 10–11-inch/25–28-cm baking pan with parchment (baking) paper. Soak the raisins in the Marsala for 30 minutes until plump. Drain, reserving the Marsala. Push the ricotta through a sieve or process with a stick blender and mix it with the sugar until smooth. Stir in the flour, reserved Marsala, egg yolks, cream, and lemon zest.

In a separate bowl, whisk the egg whites with the lemon juice to stiff peaks and fold into the ricotta mixture.

Reserving a small portion for the lattice, roll out the pastry on a lightly floured surface into a disk and line the bottom and sides of the baking pan with it. Fill with the ricotta mixture. Cut the reserved pastry into strips and arrange in a lattice pattern on top. Bake for about 1 hour. Remove, rest it for 5 minutes, then serve warm.

PANINI DOLCI AL CIOCCOLATO

LITTLE CHOCOLATE BUNS

EASY

- Preparation time: *10 minutes*
- Cooking time: *35–40 minutes*
- Calories per serving: *230*
- *Serves 6*

INGREDIENTS

- 6 tablespoons (3 oz/80 g)
  butter
- ½ cup (2½ oz/60 g)
  all-purpose (plain) flour
- 2 eggs
- scant ½ cup (1½ oz/40 g)
  hot chocolate powder
- whipped cream, to serve

Preheat the oven to 200°C/400°F/Gas Mark 6 and butter a sheet of baking parchment. Place this on a baking sheet.

Put 4 tablespoons (2 oz/50 g) of the butter into a saucepan with ⅔ cup (5 fl oz/150 ml) cold water and heat gently until the butter has melted, then bring to a boil and remove from the heat. Immediately add all the flour to the saucepan, stirring vigorously until the mixture comes away cleanly from the sides of the pan. Let cool a little, then beat in the eggs, one at a time, followed by the hot chocolate powder.

Using 2 teaspoons or a piping (pastry) bag fitted with a ½-inch/1-cm nozzle (tip), pipe 12 or more small mounds of the batter on the baking sheet. Bake for 10 minutes, then increase the temperature to 425°F/220°C/Gas Mark 7 for another 20 minutes. Remove from the oven, let cool, and serve with whipped cream.

SPONGATA DI PONTREMOLI
SPONGATA FROM PONTREMOLI

EASY

– Preparation time: *1 hour*
  + 12 hours for resting
– Cooking time: *30–35 minutes*
– Calories per serving: *551*
– *Serves 8*

FOR THE FILLING

– scant 1 cup (7 oz/200 g) clear honey
– ¼ cup (2 fl oz/50 ml) white wine
– ½ cup (2 oz/60 g) pine nuts
– ⅓ cup (2 oz/60 g) golden raisins (sultanas)
– scant 1 cup (3 ½ oz/100 g) dry cookies (biscuits), crushed
– 1 teaspoon bitter cocoa powder

FOR THE PASTRY

– 2 ⅓ cup (11 oz/300 g) all-purpose (plain) flour
– 1½ cup (3½ oz/100 g) sugar
– 1¼ sticks (5 oz/150 g) butter, softened
– 3 tablespoons white wine
– 1 egg, beaten

Make the filling by gently heating the honey with the wine. When runny, add the pine nuts, golden raisins (sultanas), crushed cookies (biscuits), and cocoa powder. Mix everything together well, transfer to a bowl, and let it rest in a cool place overnight.

The following day, preheat the oven to 350°F/180°C/ Gas Mark 4 and line a baking sheet with parchment (baking) paper.

Make the dough by combining together the flour, sugar, softened butter, and wine. Knead together well until a smooth dough is formed, then divide into two equal pieces. Roll out the first piece into a disk about ¼ inch/½ cm thick and place it on the prepared baking sheet.

Add the filling to the middle of the pastry and spread evenly leaving a border of about ¾ inch/2 cm. Roll out the remaining piece of dough into a disk of the same dimension and place this on top. Seal together the edges by crimping them with your finger and thumb. Brush with a beaten egg and make a few holes on top with the end of a spoon. Bake for 30–35 minutes. Let cool and serve.

Recipe Notes

Butter should always
be unsalted.

Eggs and fruits are assumed
to be large (UK: medium) size,
unless otherwise specified.

Milk is always whole, unless
otherwise specified.

Cooking and preparation
times are for guidance only,
as individual ovens vary.
If using a fan oven, follow
the manufacturer's
instructions concerning
oven temperatures.

Some recipes include
raw or very lightly cooked
eggs. These should be
avoided particularly by
the elderly, infants, pregnant
women, convalescents,
and anyone with an impaired
immune system.

All spoon measurements
are level. 1 teaspoon = 5 ml;
1 tablespoon = 15 ml.
Australian standard
tablespoons are 20 ml,
so Australian readers are
advised to use 3 teaspoons
in place of 1 tablespoon
when measuring small
quantities.

Cup, metric, and imperial
measurements are given
throughout, and us
equivalents are given in
brackets. Follow one set
of measurements, not
a mixture, as they are
not interchangeable.

Phaidon Press Limited
Regent's Wharf
All Saints Street
London N1 9PA

Phaidon Press Inc.
65 Bleecker Street
New York, NY 10014

www.phaidon.com

First published 2015
© 2015 Phaidon Press Limited

ISBN: 978 07148 7003 8

Italian Cooking School Desserts originates from *Il cucchiaio d'argento
estate*, first published in 2005; *Il cucchiaio d'argento cucina regionale*,
first published in 2008; *Scuola di cucina Crostate, ciambelle e biscotti*,
first published in 2013. © Editoriale Domus S.p.A. and Cucchiaio
d'Argento S.r.l.

A CIP catalogue record for this book is available from
the British Library.

Commissioning Editor: Emilia Terragni
Project Editor: Michelle Lo
Production Controller: Mandy Mackie
Designed by Atlas

Photography © Phaidon Press: Liz and Max Haarala Hamilton 6, 8,
12, 21, 22, 25, 26, 33, 49, 50, 55, 58, 60, 62, 65, 69 (steps only), 70,
80, 82, 85, 87, 90, 93, 94, 97, 101, 117, 121, 122, 125, 125, 129, 130,
134, 146, 150, 153, 154, 157, 158, 165, 166, 170; Edward Park 45, 53,
173; Andy Sewell 89

Photography © Editoriale Domus S.p.A. and Cucchiaio
d'Argento S.r.l.: Archivio Cucchiaio d'Argento s.r.l. 11, 15, 18, 28,
30, 34, 37, 38, 40, 42, 46, 57, 69 (cake only), 73, 74, 77, 78, 98, 104,
106, 109, 110, 113, 114, 118, 133, 137, 138, 141, 144, 149, 158, 161,
162, 169

Printed in Romania

The publisher would like to thank Carmen Figini, Ellie Smith,
Astrid Stavro, Nuria Cabrera, Katie Blinman, Laura Gladwin,
Theresa Bebbington, Susan Spaull, and Vanessa Bird for their
contributions to the book.